Praise for:

From Matron To
MARTYR

"Lynley Smith's work is important, and inspirational, a reminder that God's plan for this world is very much a work in progress, and that we ignore it at our peril. From a literary point of view, it's a detective story, and a fine one at that."

—Ian Wishart
Best-selling author of *Air Con, The Divinity Code, Eve's Bite* and the editor of *Investigate Magazine*

"Lynley Smith's *From Matron to Martyr* is a touching and personal account of the life of Jane Haining. This fitting tribute to a fine Christian woman rightfully keeps the memory of Jane Haining's lamp burning. Jane is one more example of decent Christianity prepared to lay down its life for the Jewish people."

—Nigel Woodley
New Zealand pastor Nigel Woodley, a dedicated supporter of Israel, published *Holocaust Exposed: The Bible Enigma* in 2009.

JANE HAINING'S ULTIMATE
SACRIFICE FOR THE JEWS

FROM MATRON TO MARTYR

Lynley Smith

 Zaccmedia

Published by Zaccmedia
www.zaccmedia.com
info@zaccmedia.com

Published July 2017

ISBN: 978-1-911211-35-8

British Library Cataloguing-in-Publication Data
A catalogue record for this book is available from the British Library.

Zaccmedia aims to produce books that will help to extend and build up the Kingdom of God. We do not necessarily agree with every view expressed by the authors, or with every interpretation of Scripture expressed. We expect readers to make their own judgment in the light of their understanding of God's Word and in an attitude of Christian love and fellowship.

This novel is a work of fiction. However, many names, descriptions, entities, and incidents included in the story are based on the lives of real people. Fictitious names are marked with an asterisk.

Dedication

I dedicate this book to the workers for the harvest: to Grace, Bruce, and the many others who supported me as I travelled, researched, prayed, and wrote; to Sharon and the other intercessors who wept over this story; and to my Jewish friends who have encouraged me to add this small portion to the history books of their nation.

Yes, indeed! I tell you that unless a grain of wheat that falls to the ground dies, it stays just a grain; but if it dies, it produces a big harvest.

John 12:24 (cjb)

Acknowledgments

I am indebted to the late Reverend David McDougall for his thorough biography, *Jane Haining 1897 - 1944*, first printed in 1949, and edited and updated in 1998 by Ian Alexander. I am also indebted to the Church of Scotland World Mission, publishers of this booklet, who have given me permission to source much valuable information from it.

Thanks also to Nicholas Railton, author of *Jane Haining and the Work of the Scottish Mission with Hungarian Jews, 1932 – 1945;* copyright Nicholas Railton, 2007; ISBN 978-963-7893-32-2, for permitting me to source valuable background information from his in-depth study of the Church of Scotland's mission to Hungary and Jane Haining's part in this.

Table of Contents

Foreword

"Never again," have been the watchwords for Jews ever since the Nazis exterminated six million Jewish people—burning them in ovens, shooting them, and experimenting with their bodies.

Now, with anti-Semitism increasing in the world, with denials that the Holocaust ever happened, with antipathy toward Israel increasing, I am most pleased that this book exists. If ever there was a time for someone to help us remember that there really were people, Christian people, who stood with us during our darkest hours, it is now. Jews need to know that true followers of Jesus are our friends.

Imagine a Jewish man being marched into an oven by someone who regularly wore a cross and went to church on Sunday. How confusing it must have been to sort out how this Christian neighbour could betray him. Since that era, it's been difficult for Jews to distinguish between a person who truly follows the Messiah of Israel and someone who merely professes to do so. That's why this book is important. It shows the sort of Christian behaviour that makes Jews feel safer around Christians and their message of salvation.

The following quotation, taken from the *Yad Vashem* website makes the point:

I believe that it was really due to Lorenzo that I am alive today; and not so much for his material aid, as for his having constantly reminded me by his presence...that there still existed a just world outside our own, something and someone still pure and whole...for which it was worth surviving.

> Primo Levi describes his rescuer,
> Lorenzo Perrone (*If This Is A Man*)

Perhaps the best-known rescuer is Oscar Schindler, whom Steven Spielberg made famous in his powerful movie, *Schindler's List*. Schindler, a successful businessman, made it possible for many Jews to escape Hitler's persecution.

Yet there were many others who took a stand, willing to hide Jewish people and even die with our people, who go unrecognised. Many of these righteous Gentiles are remembered along the Avenue of the Righteous Among the Nations, leading into the *Yad Vashem* memorial building in Jerusalem. Although many names are presented there, not all the Christians who hid and protected my people, many dying with our people, are mentioned. Yet anyone who visits this avenue gets the sense that there were a host of people who were with us. One of them is Jane Haining.

If you're Jewish, remember that this woman did what she did because she was following the teachings of Jesus (*Yeshua* in Hebrew), who laid down his life for the people to whom he came first, the Jews. She was following his footsteps, sacrificing herself because of her love for the God of Abraham, Isaac and Jacob; for his Anointed One, the Messiah; and for his people, Israel.

If you're a Christian, let this book challenge you to love those whom God loved: his first-born, Israel, i.e., the Jews. Don't believe the lies spoken against us, as was so often the case in pre-war

Germany. Those who persecuted my people, often sending them to their deaths, were the same who also named the name of Jesus every Christmas and Easter and possibly also on Sundays. But they didn't truly follow him or they would have loved, not hated, his own people.

> May I encourage you to stand with the physical family of the Messiah in these dark and dangerous days. May the story of Jane Haining give you the courage and confidence to say along with the Jewish people, "Never again!"

—Barry Rubin

Rabbi Barry Rubin has served Emmanuel Messianic Jewish Congregation since 1981. He has been president and CEO of Messianic Jewish Communications, a messianic publisher, and distributor of Messianic Jewish Resources, since 1988. Both organizations are located in Clarksville, Maryland, USA.

Introduction

As time moves on and memories of the darkest years of European history dim, there is a growing movement among writers, historians, and filmmakers to record for posterity the grim events of the World War II period.

This is not done from a ghoulish desire to rehash atrocities of the past, but rather from a desire to bring some sort of cathartic understanding of what transpired in those days and what it might mean to our generation and those to come.

As a journalist, I quickly learned that every person was a story, and if told well, that story could be beneficial to the readers in some way. In other words, every person's life was a message for those around them and for generations to come. As a Christian journalist, I learned to look deeper to try to understand the spiritual implications of each life I investigated.

As I contemplated writing this book, I came to realise that the message in the life of the unassuming Scottish missionary, Jane Haining, was a message that could be missed by those who simply saw her as a courageous lady who stubbornly refused to leave her post and, as a result, died as a martyr during World War II at the hands of the Nazis. No, I believe this story has far greater implications than that.

It was the call of God on my life to follow the trail set by her story, to discover for myself who this woman was, how she came to be in such a place to make such a sacrifice, and what she may have felt as she found her life moving irrevocably towards a horrifying death.

My journey was both a physical and spiritual one. While travelling in her footsteps, visiting the places in which she had lived, talking to those who knew something of her, researching and consulting, I came to see clearly the hand of God in my every move. Bizarrely, someone from the farthest ends of the earth (from New Zealand) found herself making this pilgrimage, and in so doing, experiencing the illumination of His light on this previously obscure but profoundly touching life.

As I travelled, I began to form a progressively clearer picture of this lady and discovered, to my amazement, the many parallels in our lives. Our many character and personality traits in common resulted in my choosing many of the same activities to pursue as Jane Haining had. For instance, I preferred to spend much of my time working for the community and especially for children in the community.

Because of this I felt peculiarly equipped to write this story. I could put myself in Jane's shoes and imagine how she felt, how she thought. It will not surprise the reader to discover that I am a distant relative of Jane Haining—very distant as far as I can discern, but nevertheless having enough of the family DNA to be able to pick her out from others in an old group photo hanging on a wall in Budapest.

There is no evidence that Jane kept a diary, but I have chosen a fictional diary format for the story to bring a personal touch and to show the transitions in Jane's life from a young child with a raw faith to a great woman of God seeking His deeper revelation and wisdom. I have set the scene with a short account of my journey to Europe to discover for myself just who this lady was, the environments in which she lived, and the impact her life has had on the generations that have followed her in these places.

One thing that became apparent as I travelled was that her memory will not die. Wherever I went, there was someone who had guarded a small part of her history, a remnant of people from each segment of her life from the little village of Dunscore in Scotland through to the magnificent city of Budapest in Hungary, who had faithfully, and with surprising passion, kept their small portion of her memory alive. It seems they sensed that the true value of this woman's life was yet to be fully revealed. My great desire is to draw these threads together into a compelling story, worthy of the attention of this generation, both Jew and Gentile.

I have tried to include as much accurate historical detail as possible on Jane's life, as appropriate to the story, but further historical information may be found in the extensive appendices. Most names and places used in the story are factual, with fictional names annotated as such.

I invite the reader to join me on this journey, this pilgrimage, this unfolding of an incredible story of God's all-embracing love for his creation, and especially for His chosen people, and the way he demonstrated it through the life and actions of a humble and obedient woman.

PART ONE:
A STORY UNFOLDS

His Purposes Revealed

It all began with a small booklet—one that you would not take a second look at really. But this booklet was drawn to my attention in rather special circumstances.

I climbed wearily into my car and headed south. It had been a long day at the office, and deadlines were fast approaching. There were still several stories to write, including a front page story, and no one else to pick up the slack.

But family was family, and my duty and desire was to spend as much time with my elderly and ailing mother as possible as she journeyed through her last weeks of life in the city hospital.

This visit was different. Mum was alert and waiting for me. On her bed lay a booklet published by the Church of Scotland, which I vaguely remembered having seen before but had disregarded as of little interest.

"Read it," she whispered. Her voice had all but gone, and the effort of speaking was almost too much these days. "She is a relative of ours."

I took the little booklet and leafed through it, noting its amateurish typesetting and presentation, with photocopied photographs. Throughout were handwritten jottings, made by my already deceased aunt, and a note in the front indicating a probable family connection to the person who was the subject of the booklet.

I popped the booklet into my bag, thinking I'd look at it after I got my next paper out. I was working on a weekly newspaper, and there was always a day of downtime before the mad dash to gather stories and photos for the next edition. My mum had always been interested in family history, and, while mostly accurate in her research, had come up with some slightly suspect links such as our connection to Bonny Prince Charlie, based on the flimsy evidence of our Scottish heritage and a few surnames in common in the family line. So this was probably another of those punts. No hurry to investigate this one.

In fact, the booklet lay on my desk until after my mother's funeral several months later before I picked it up and looked seriously at it. I opened it and began to read. The effect was astounding.

Page after page recounted the life of someone I'd never heard of, but whose story was gripping to the point that I could not put the booklet down. I read and reread it many times. I had read a lot of biographies and had the privilege of researching and writing many stories, but none touched me like this one. A most odd thing was happening. I actually felt I was within the story, living it with the heroine—sharing her passions, her emotions, her concerns, and her fears. I felt her strong faith, and I recognised many of her personality traits. In some ways it was like reading a story about myself set in another time, another place, with other circumstances. I related to this woman. The story was set in Hungary, a country that had never before taken my interest. It was the story of one woman's ultimate sacrifice for the Jews.

My imagination had been aroused, and questions began to form in my mind. Who would do such a thing and why? Did she know what she was doing—did she have a choice? Was her death a deliberate act of sacrifice or simply the culmination of a set of evil circumstances beyond her control? Could she foresee the outcome of her actions before it was too late to escape? At what point did it become apparent to her that she was to forfeit her life? Clearly I had to dig deeper into the story, and equally clearly, I had to get up and go to do so.

Extraordinary circumstances require extraordinary responses. So in the middle of 2009, I booked myself a round-the-world ticket and headed out to follow in the footsteps of Jane Haining, the heroine of that little booklet. My goal was to talk to as many people as I could who might shed some light on her life—a tall order perhaps, given that more than sixty-five years had passed since her death, and many of those who had known her well were already deceased. I also wanted to visit the places where Jane had grown up, worked, and died, to see for myself something of the reality of her daily life.

My first stop was in the little village of Dunscore and the delightful town of Dumfries in Scotland. It was here that Jane grew up, attending the local Dunscore school and then moving on to become a boarder at the prestigious Dumfries Academy.

Next I visited Glasgow, where Jane trained in business studies and entered the work force. She also moved into leadership roles in her local church, Queens Park West Church, as a Sunday school teacher and a missions volunteer in the local community. A visit to Edinburgh, where Jane trained as a missionary in preparation for her appointment by the Church of Scotland Mission to Budapest Girls' Home, followed.

My next destination was Budapest, where Jane spent the most meaningful years of her life, caring for Jewish and Gentile girls during the difficult and dangerous pre-war and war years. Here she held the post of matron at the Church of Scotland's Scottish Mission Girls' Home.

But my journey would be in no way complete unless I took that final step—the journey from Budapest to Krakow and the Auschwitz Concentration Camp in Poland, where Jane lost her life.

Of course, I had to go by train as she had. This excursion turned out to be quite an adventure for me with several big challenges. A major snow storm, which made Europe grind to a halt, cast doubt on the ability of the overnight train to reach its destination at all. Then, on the return journey, one of the train's passenger carriages actually caught fire. I did arrive back in Budapest safely and only a few hours late. While these challenges made my journey interesting, to say the least, they rank as insignificant alongside those experienced by our heroine as she travelled to her death.

I was drawn back to Budapest in October, 2010, just ten months after my first visit, to a conference commemorating Jane Haining. There I was be greeted by a most unexpected surprise. Reverend Aaron Stevens, minister at Jane's church, the Church of Scotland's St Columba's Church on Vörösmarty utca, had just discovered a Bible and an old book about English plants tucked away under other items in a very old safe on the church premises. The Bible had been presented to Jane by her Sunday school teachers in 1931, and the plant book was a prize she had received from Dumfries Academy.

It is anyone's guess just how long those two books had remained hidden from sight in the safe, which possibly dated back to the war years, and it made me wonder what other mementos of her life might still come to light.

* * *

February, 2017: My presentiment proved to be prophetic. The Postscript, at the end of this story reveals amazing further recent discoveries, since the publication of the first edition of this book.

It seems the story of Jane Haining is still unfolding...

PART TWO:
JANE HAINING—
THE FORMATIVE YEARS

Prologue:
View from the Summit

There it is—my name, Jane Mathison Haining, just as I had imagined it would be. How incredible this is. It is exactly as we were taught on earth—a book, the Book of Life, and names, thousands upon thousands of them. And there is mine among them, beautifully inscribed in gold.

I take time to look around me. The horror of the past few days, weeks even, has dropped off me like a loosely fitting cloak. I'm suddenly totally free from all cares, anxieties, fears—not that I would have allowed anyone to see those. I'm a free spirit at long last. I'm me, and I'm totally accepted as such. I know that in the past, some would have described me as a little bossy and overly sensible, but this is no source for concern here. In this place, I can already see that grace extends far beyond our individual differences and idiosyncrasies.

My eyes fasten on a group of people. Can I call them people any longer? They are milling around as if waiting for something important to happen. Do I know any of them? Funnily enough they seem familiar to me but I can't recall actually having met them on earth. Nevertheless, there is a rapport, and I'm drawn into the crowd.

A touch on my elbow, a friendly smile, and I become one of this heavenly group. How easy it is to gain its membership. How unlike what I had seen on earth, where my dear children, the ones whom I cared for, were excluded, ostracised, and tormented simply because they were Jews.

We are standing on an expansive lawn, surrounded by meadows in which myriads of wild flowers are dancing in tune to something that must be a gentle wind, though I can't actually feel any wind. In the distance I can see what looks like a beautiful city, or at least an accumulation of buildings that shine and sparkle in a radiant light despite the fact that there is no sun and no shadows. I'm mesmerised by the sight.

We do not have to wait for very long. We become aware of a small group of beings, maybe five or six, approaching us. I would describe them as almost floating effortlessly towards us. Surely these are the angels I have heard so much about but have never seen with my own eyes on earth. Certainly I had known them to exist and had even felt their presence around me, especially in those horrific last days in Auschwitz. Their presence was almost tangible there. I could discern exactly where they stood by a strange but pleasant warmth emanating from them. It comforted me enormously.

Now I'm seeing them with my own eyes, and they certainly fulfil every expectation— and more. How I would have loved to see on earth these heavenly creatures as some report to have done. But now I can feast on this radiant sight, and here the experience isn't transient.

The group is being beckoned to move along a sandy path across the lawn that leads towards the city, which looms larger and larger as we approach until it reaches unlimited proportions. There is nothing in my previous experience that can compare with this or help me understand it. We enter through a gate in the wall around the city and find ourselves walking on a golden road lined with houses and buildings of every kind imaginable— and trees, beautiful trees. How I love the way they tower over us with their intricate patterns of interconnecting branches and leaves in an artist's palette of colours.

We stop in a square and wander around, looking in wonder at the surrounding buildings. Budapest's Andrássy út (avenue) with its fine statues and ornate buildings has nothing on this, nor does my beloved Glasgow or the jewel in Scotland's crown, Edinburgh.

I become aware of a new presence, even more dazzling than the angelic beings. Overcome, I find myself bowing, then kneeling, and then lying flat on my face before this presence. I'm lost in the wonder of it and quite unaware of how I actually came to be lying on the ground. I gradually realise that not only I but all those with me have fallen prostrate, and a voice, something like the chiming of bells embodying all the harmonies in the world, is speaking to us, each of us, individually.

We all know we have met our Maker. We are in His presence. There are no words to explain this experience, no superlatives which even start to describe it. It is outside of our earthly, rational mind-set and, as such, is accessible only to those who come here. Our little taste of heaven we yearn for on earth is a mere shadow of the real thing.

What amazes me most is that I find I am now conversing with this great God who has saved me despite my unworthiness. He is reaching into me, to the core of my being, and I sense an intimate love like that of a mother—something my soul has been thirsting for since my own mother died when I was only five years old, something I had tried so hard to give those poor little orphaned and unwanted Hungarian Jewish girls. He is restoring things, making all things new.

Now I am complete.

But I am still me, and I have a list of questions. The foremost, the one that goaded me unmercifully, especially as I lay on my bunk at night in the concentration camp barracks, comes immediately to mind. Back then, I would ask, "Why, Lord, have you let this happen to me? Why have you cut my life short and taken me away from my children who need me so much? Why have you allowed the wicked to prosper in this place? Why, why, why? I thought my life had a purpose. I've dedicated my life to help those little ones. Where is the sense in cutting that short, especially when the job is not finished and they face ever increasing danger? Will my death also have a purpose, perhaps a more important one, than my life had? Are You, God, allowing me to suffer this fate for Your greater purpose?"

In the holiest of places, all this spills out before my God in random heart cries as I struggle to make sense of it all. Just as I have sensed the healing love flow from Him, I sense His reply that my death is indeed of great import and holds a very special message that someday will be vital for those who receive it. The blood spilt, my blood willingly sacrificed, has more power than all my years of sacrificial work in the Budapest orphanage.

I boldly respond, for I have never been accused of being timid in the face of authority! I'm simply not prepared to let this issue rest so easily. "But God, how is it that you took me to be with you at such a crucial time, when my children were facing greater dangers than could ever have been imagined? How could you do that? Why didn't you wait until they had been rescued?"

God is not the least bit fazed by my accusatory outburst. "It is I who has your times and seasons in My hand," He answers with a gentle smile. "I brought you to Budapest. I watched over you during those years of hardship, and it was I who led you on to make the great sacrifice you made. This was no accident. From the beginning, I trained you to fulfill this mission, and from the beginning your heart was open and willing, although in your wildest imagination you would not have dreamed of the outcome. Do you know how precious your humble obedience has been to Me?"

"But, God!" I begin. I'm as stubborn as ever—some things don't change. I'm still grappling with the thought that I had to leave my children in their hour of need. "What's the point of it all? You are not random in what You do. There must be a purpose. How can my death benefit those children and their families?" My practical mind is working overtime, and finally it hits me. My story is not finished because it has not been told! My mission is incomplete.

With a confidence and conviction that matches, or even betters, that with which I addressed my Nazi accusers in Budapest, I demand action. "My story must be told," I say.

"And so it shall be," He replies.

At last I am at peace.

Early Days in Dunscore

School Assignment Written by Jane Haining,

Eleven Years Old, 1908

I wish teachers could think of other more interesting topics for us to write about at the start of the year. I am fast becoming wearied by repeated demands to tell about my family and my childhood as though I'm already an adult. I'm only eleven. My story has some sad moments I don't actually want to recall and write about—certainly not each year! So it's with a big sigh and some resignation I start this story. Here it goes!

I was born in 1897 in the little village of Dunscore, about ten miles from the large and exciting (to my eyes) town of Dumfries. My father, Thomas Haining, married my mother, Jane Mathison, in 1890. Mother came from Kirkcudbrightshire on the coast about twenty-five miles from Dunscore. Father brought her back to live at Lochenhead farm, at Throughgate, less than a mile from the village.

It is the loveliest little village—not so little actually—with lots of shops and businesses, including a butcher, a haberdasher, a tailor, a church, and a school. The town is bursting with families. Everyone seems to have big families, so our family with three girls is one of the smaller ones. People mostly live in white, two-storey, row houses neatly lining the narrow streets in the village, although there are also many families just like ours, scattered around on farms within walking distance of the village.

Our town is nestled in a fertile valley crisscrossed with little stone walls and hedges and overlooked by steep, rather barren hills, which look really pretty, covered in their moss and heather. I love it when I get the opportunity to walk up there with my father or some of the other village children, as it has become a special place to me. But I don't often get the chance.

My father owns Lochenhead Farm and some other houses in the village. I was born in the farm cottage in the top, left, front bedroom. The cottage is quite close to the main road, and is surrounded by large barns for the animals.

I walk down to the village every weekday to attend Dunscore School, which is a stone building with several classrooms and is only just big enough for all the students that attend.

Miss Sloane has been my teacher for quite a few years, and I like her a lot. She is very strict and demands instant obedience. I think this strictness is necessary for a school teacher, and if I ever take on that job, I imagine I will also be strict but fair.

Despite that, I find her to be very kind. She seems to have taken a special interest in me, especially in encouraging me to read and read and read. It doesn't take too much encouragement, as I devour a book with the appetite of one who hasn't eaten for a year—all sorts of books, but I like biographies of famous and brave people best.

Our headmaster, Mr. Gold, is also a great teacher, and I think he gets special pleasure out of seeing how I love to study, whereas some other students really just want to play at school. There is not a subject that doesn't interest me. Mr. Gold is encouraging me to apply for a scholarship to attend the Dumfries Academy next year, and I'm determined to win that.

Life hasn't always been easy for me in Dunscore, despite the idyllic setting. At home, there have been so many sad times. My oldest sister, Alison, was born in 1891. Then my mother had twin boys, James and Thomas, but they both died four months later. I think my mother grieved about that for a long time, as she often looked sadly at me when we talked about those days. Two little photos hold pride of place on our living room mantle piece as reminders of the boys.

In 1895, my sister Margaret was born. She is exactly two years, four months, and six days older than me. When I was little, I used to love to give people the exact age gap when they asked me about our ages. They didn't expect a small child to know things with such accuracy.

It was so nice to have two older sisters, but especially Margaret, as we could play a lot of games together. By the time I was four years old, I was starting to boss her, but she didn't mind at all. We were very good playmates. We would spend lots of time after she got home from school wandering around the farm, playing imaginary games, climbing trees, and finding all sorts of tiny creatures to bring home to keep in a jar in our bedroom. Alison mostly had chores to do in the house after school, but Margaret and I made the most of those years when we were free to run around and play wherever we wanted.

After I turned five, two very traumatic things happened. I had only been going to school for two months when my mother gave birth to another baby. The whole thing had been fascinating me, and I was dying to see the new baby. I was hoping for a little brother to replace the two Mum was so sad about. I arrived home from school that day with my sisters to find the house frantic. People seemed to be running everywhere, and we children were told to shush and go and play outside. My grown-up cousin was there along with the local midwife and several other relatives, and Father was walking around with a look on his face I'd never seen before.

It scared me. At five years old, I, who loved to put everything in order, wasn't up to coping with whatever was going on. I went outside and found a place to hide in the woodshed to nurse my fears and apprehensions. Today, of course, I would have been able to cope much better.

From my hiding place, I heard the *clip clop* of a horse heading at speed to the house and hushed, urgent, male voices. I recognised the voice of our village doctor. I just waited in the woodshed, feeling miserable and confused, until my sister came and found me and led me back inside. I don't know how much later that was.

Father was there and so were all the other people. Lily, our household help, was sitting in an armchair holding the tiniest baby I had ever seen, rocking it and cooing to it, but tears were streaming down her face. There was a strange silence, except for the odd sob from Lily, and Father was looking like he was about to cry too. I ran to him and threw my arms around him, looking up into his face for reassurance. He just wrapped his arms around me and rocked me for what seemed like a very long time before he told me that Mother was very sick and the doctor was with her.

The next few hours were a blur. I think someone got something for me and my sisters to eat, and then we were packed off to bed upstairs. We huddled together and no one slept. Finally, Father came up to our room with the saddest news a five-year old could ever hear. Mother had died, despite the best efforts of the doctor.

I didn't understand it, didn't realise that it wouldn't be all better in the morning, but my older sisters certainly did. We just clung to each other and to Father. He was crying now too.

I remember our conversation vividly, even though it is years later.

"When is Mother going to get up?" I demanded, looking from one sister to the other and then to Father, wondering who would read me my night time story. "When..." my voice trailed off as I saw the unfathomable expressions on their faces.

"Mother won't be getting up, little one," Father said gently, holding me close. "She has gone to heaven. Our precious Lord has taken her to live in that wonderful place where she will never be sick again. We will see her again in heaven. But, in the meantime, you have a lovely new baby sister, and you must be a big, brave girl and help to look after her." He tried unsuccessfully to stifle some more sobs. I was frightened and very confused.

It took many weeks for us to recover from this nightmare event, if we ever did recover. The village people were very kind, with the women dropping off home baking and the men offering to lend a hand on the farm. The house seemed to be full of bunches of flowers brought in by neighbours. But nothing could replace my mother, who had run the household like clockwork. I think I missed her more than anyone. I missed our cuddles each night, the stories she read to us, the funny nicknames she called us, and that warm knee I could always climb on when I had scraped my leg playing some vigorous game or other around the farmyard. I was only five!

Father found solace over time in his very strong faith. People described both my parents as very God fearing, and we learned to be too. We attended the Craig Free Church every Sunday. The children remained for Sunday school afterwards. Many of the children complained about having to sit through a whole service before going out to Sunday school, but I enjoyed the solemnity of it and loved to hear the old psalms sung each week. I think those times in church and listening to Father read the Bible to us each evening helped us cope with the death of our mother.

We still go along every Sunday, and now Father is a church deacon, helping the pastor. I am learning so much about our heavenly Father, and I want so much to show others how much He loves us. Church is one of the places I like best.

It would be good to be able to say that sad times were over and we could build our lives as a family again, but another crisis arose. Our new baby sister Helen was not very strong and often caused much concern with poor feeding and constant colds. I often picked her up to comfort her when she was snuffling and crying, and she would look up to me with such a lovely smile. I wanted her to get well and strong and would have done anything I could to help her. We had all lost our mother, but she had never even known Mother. I don't think that is fair!

One day, when Helen was about eighteen months old, she got really sick, and after about one week, she died. The whole district knew about our loss within hours. Again, the village people came to help, and I know Father was very grateful. We were the talk of the town.

I overheard Mrs. Armstrong, who lives on a farm down the road, talking to our local butcher as I burst in the door on an errand to his shop. "It's such a pity, those poor wee mites, without a mother, and now without their baby sister," she said. "What's the good Lord thinking to bring such hardship on such a lovely family?"

"We won't ever understand in this lifetime," he replied. They both abruptly stopped talking as they saw me enter. I felt very strange and somehow excluded.

We had the tiniest coffin for Helen. I was now old enough to realise that death was final and that she had been taken from us permanently. That thought really troubled me, so I buried myself in my books, my games, and my Bible. I was a very good reader for my age.

I think since this time, I have become very serious about life. Daily village life has gone on with Sunday school picnics and church Christmas celebrations to look forward to. The Sunday school Christmas plays we have staged have taught me to love drama, despite my dislike of making an exhibition of myself.

We have also had the occasional trip to Dumfries, taking the pony and trap, but things on the farm are different now. With Mother gone, we girls are needed to do many more chores. When I was younger, I had to bring the firewood in after school and also feed the chickens and any lambs that had lost their mothers. There were always other chores as well. Lily left us to get married, and our cousin, Margaret, came to look after us for a while.

But, of course, they both needed our help, and we did the best we could. My after-school playtimes have long been a thing of the past. With my sisters going away to school in Dumfries and Father so busy on the farm, I now have to help with the cooking and cleaning.

One event that really caught our attention was the opening of the Dunscore railway station when the line from Moniaive to Dumfries opened in 1905. I was just eight years old, and I couldn't wait to have a chance to go on the train. But, as usual, we had to find a time when Father was not too busy on the farm, so my impatience didn't pay off.

When we did make the journey, I was very excited. Sitting in a railway carriage for the first time and watching the houses, barns, and pastures whizz by was an experience never to be forgotten. Dumfries was suddenly not so far away after all. And when I got there, I saw for the first time the school I now want so much to attend. I know many girls from the village do not go on to further education past the village school because they are needed at home, but I dream of visiting all the wonderful places I read about. And I know I must be ready to leave our village if I want to do that.

Lonely Teenage Years

Diary of Jane Haining

December, 1914

I have decided to keep a diary. I am now seventeen, and, as each year passes, I realise my life is moving forward in a pattern. I want to be able to look back in years to come and remember and understand these years. I have a sense that all I do now will have some future purpose, but I have no idea as yet what that may be.

As this is my first diary entry, I will need to go back to my first years here at Dumfries Academy. Yes, I was successful in winning a scholarship to come here, following in the footsteps of my sisters Alison and Margaret. Father and all the family were delighted with the news, but I took it in my stride, perhaps because I had always believed I would achieve this. There is much more yet to achieve.

I was one of the first boarders in the new Moat Hostel for Girls at the academy. That is an honour, I know, and I suppose we will have reunions when we leave school so we can all get together and share the funny, happy, and not-so-happy moments of our lives together in the hostel. I was also one of the first pupils to use the new junior block to the school, which was built in 1910.

Quite honestly, my first term away from home was a great shock to me. I thought I was very grown up, and in any case, I had two sisters ahead of me at this school. But I found myself missing Father terribly and missing my pet lambs, the hill paths I had wandered in the summer, and my bedroom with its familiar stuffed toys and bookcase full of my favourite books.

Suddenly I was in impersonal surroundings, sharing a dormitory with ten girls I didn't know and with not a lot of space for my possessions. My initial reaction, as always, was to go deep into myself and to find comfort in the only person who I felt really knew me—Jesus. I was growing more and more reliant on this wonderful friend, and I'm sure this afforded me a measure of stability that others have since described as maturity beyond my years. I honestly can't say when I first realised He was always there with me—it's something I have known since I felt His presence when wandering on the hills around Dunscore.

At first, I found refuge in books from the school library and spent most of my spare time lying on my bed with my nose in a book while I learnt to cope with this new hustle and bustle of hostel life. I gradually fitted into this life and began to enjoy it, with its routines and regular challenges as well as its fun and friendships.

During my second year at Moat, we went through a silly, girlie phase where all our childhood nicknames were revealed. Fortunately, my family had only called me Jean or my real name Jane, so I wasn't embarrassed by that, but some of the girls had the most ridiculous baby names, such as Tootles and Snudgie, and these were used ruthlessly for the rest of the year!

Moat Hostel is a beautiful house with polished floors and large spacious rooms—nothing like the boarding schools you could imagine from reading Charles Dickens's *Nicholas Nickleby*. The matron says it was once a hotel.

The hostel staff are strict, and there are lots of rules, such as no noise whatsoever after lights out, but they are also there for you if you have a problem or are feeling lonely. We have to be up bright and early with our beds made at six in the morning waiting to hear the breakfast bell, which lives at the bottom of the stairs and signals us to come down for breakfast. Girls take turns at ringing the bell, but I waited until almost everyone had had their turn before volunteering. A full day of lessons follows, with a cooked lunch at midday. We have a duty roster to help in setting and clearing tables.

After school, we have some free time for sports or hobbies, which I often spend in the library, and then it is time for dinner and evening prep from six to nine in the evening—juniors finish earlier.

On the weekend, we are either involved in school projects of one kind or another or are watching the boys' weekly sports events and sometimes providing afternoon tea after the final whistle. Some girls are in sports teams, and last year, I tried out for the top girls' hockey team and was surprised to be selected. I wound up with my photo in the school magazine, which delighted Father and the rest of my family. While I love games of all sorts, I haven't played many team sports.

This year, I have also helped the editor of the school magazine to sort out contributions, but I haven't contributed anything myself. I find my studies take up almost all my spare time. I have a real desire to do exceptionally well as it may be important for my future, but I still wanted to help our editor. She is making history as the first female editor of our magazine!

Several Days Later

I'm very excited. I've just been invited out to tea next Saturday by the parents of my good friend Christina* here in the hostel.

"Mother and Father want you to come to tea with us on Saturday," Christina said and added with a knowing smile, "Of course you will be interested to know both my brothers will be there too."

I blushed so red I'm sure she noticed, and I stammered a quick "thank you."

Her family is so nice, and her mother always cooks the best scones just for me! Christina also has a darling little sister and the two aforementioned older brothers, but I'm a bit too shy to talk to them!

I need to record what our lives are like in the hostel so you, diary, will understand why we get excited about being invited out to tea.

All the boarders look forward to Saturdays, as that is the only time they are allowed to be invited out for dinner or tea. I don't have relations in Dumfries, but I haven't been short of invitations to the homes of family friends and the families of my school friends. I have lots of friends, perhaps because I don't have special friends, which always makes other girls jealous; I just get on with almost all of them.

On Sundays, we walk in a long crocodile formation down to the church on Buccleuch Street, not far at all from the academy. At first, I was embarrassed by this as I know some of the young boys in the town were laughing at us as we walked by and calling us silly names, but I soon realised their mocking was of no consequence; our group far outnumbered them in any case. There is safety in numbers they say. It took a while to get used to, but now I'm proud of my school uniform, which of course we wear whenever we go out. And I'm very proud of my school.

On Sunday afternoons, the teachers take us out for a walk around the town in our famous crocodile, sometimes to show us historic sites. Dumfries is full of history. Some very important events took place here, including the victory of Robert the Bruce over his archenemy John Comyn, opening the door to his becoming the greatest king of Scotland. You can visit the site where he killed Comyn at Greyfriars Church and the site of Dumfries Castle at Castledykes where he raised the royal standard after the English justices surrendered to him there. He grew up in the Dumfries and Galloway area.

Dumfries is full of history and I really enjoy these outings. But of course we can only go on them in good weather, which in Dumfries means mostly in the summer months.

There are also special weekends and holidays when we can get leave to go home. I always look forward to it, but not so much in the past couple of years. At first, I couldn't wait to get home to see all the familiar things and sleep again in my own bedroom. I also used to catch up with my friends in the village. But lately, things have changed. Some of my friends have moved to other areas and others, who haven't gone on to further their education, seem to me now to have a much narrower view of life than I do. Some are more interested in boys, and some are even thinking of getting married.

I remember a conversation a couple of months ago with my best friend from the village, Helen, not my deceased sister but another Helen. "What are you going to do next year?" I asked, wondering where her life would lead her, as I was just beginning to mull over all the possibilities for my own life.

"I don't know. Just probably stay around here, and maybe I can find someone to marry," she answered.

"Is that all you want to do?" I asked.

"What else is there?" she returned with a look of surprise on her face. I was shocked, as I had shared with her some of my hopes and dreams for an exciting life, assuming all young people had these.

I think my years away from home must have changed me. That worries me, as I don't know if I fit in at home any more. When I go home, I find my family is much the same. I pick up some of my old jobs, but for me, it isn't really the same. I find myself longing for the hustle and bustle of the hostel, even though I'm the least "hustlely and bustlely" person in it. I think I'm between two worlds.

In this diary, I should make mention of my school achievements to date. My family is very proud of these, and I take a certain quiet pride in them too, but I never let them dominate my opinion of myself. I believe the Bible is correct when it teaches that character is more important than achievements, that in times of testing it is your character that brings you through successfully and not past accomplishments.

I know these are not the usual thoughts for someone as young as I, but all my life I have been aware that the superficial is also transitory. I am looking for something deeper.

So, in my first year here, I received seven prizes at prize-giving, including firsts in Latin, French, and English. I love languages and find them really easy, but I don't have any difficulty with the other subjects either. I have gained prizes every year since then, not quite so many, but still, more than any other student I think.

While all that is very satisfying, I must say I get the most satisfaction out of being a senior student buddy to the new students. My sisters have left the academy, so I am the sole representative of my family here now. I think I have become more mature and more responsible. I know how the new girls feel—far away from home and, in a way, motherless, so I have volunteered for the past two years to be one of the team that introduces the new girls to the hostel. That means sitting with them at meal times, checking up on how they are getting on, popping into their dorm after school for a chat, and helping them sort out their squabbles. Girls really squabble a lot, especially when they are about thirteen or fourteen, and they can say really hurtful things to each other. I have even asked if I can sleep in the dorm with a really homesick girl in her first week at school, and the matron has allowed this— but only for a week. She says the girls must get used to being with their own age group as soon as possible.

February, 1915

Diary, for the first time in my life, I have encountered a problem I don't know how to avoid or solve. It can be summed up in one word—boys! I can't dismiss them any more as unimportant or in the ignore category. Something dreadful has happened, well actually, two dreadful things have happened, and I'm at a loss to know what to do.

Firstly, my friends at the hostel, all of them, have suddenly become boy crazy, and that is all they talk about. I am not a very outgoing person, and it quite honestly scares me to think I should be behaving like that too. I don't want to, but if I don't, I'm afraid I won't have much in common any more with the other girls in Moat House. They will think I'm an old maid at the tender age of seventeen and a half!

The second dreadful thing is that I recently found I could no longer read the blackboard comfortably and had to have my eyes checked in town. The optician gave me a set of eye glasses, which I hate. I have to wear them, during class at least, so I try to sit in the back row in most classes so no one can see when I put them on. I'm convinced they make me look like an old maid, and this will finally convince my friends I really am one. I am very upset about this but don't know who to turn to for help.

Our hostel matron has said I'm being silly to worry about it. "Men make passes at girls in glasses!" she said with a poker face.

I just felt she was laughing at me. Whatever will the people in the village think if they see me with my glasses on? They already call me "the scholar" and other names adults think are fine but that make students cringe. When I am an adult, I will be especially kind to anyone who has to wear eye glasses.

June, 1915

How remiss of me. Life has been so busy with end-of-year exams, preparations for the future, and, of course, farewell parties in our dorms for us final-year students who will soon leave here and go in different directions, that I have forgotten my diary.

I have got over my anti-eye glasses phase—well almost! If there is a handsome young man around, I still forget to put them on, despite the classroom blackboard being a bit of a blur.

To summarise the past several months, one word will do—*study!* But the reward was well worth it. I received the Modern Dux award. This award is for those taking languages. Another student was awarded the Classical Dux award, which is of equal value. The school held an awards afternoon, and a huge crowd of people, including Father and my sisters, turned up. It was a bit daunting. I was very nervous because I suspected I would win this prize. It has been my goal for several years now, but you never really know until your name is called out. Fortunately, we didn't have to give a speech. The head of school took on that responsibility, so I merely had to walk up, receive my award, and say a quick thank you.

The school headmaster made some very kind comments about my achievements. "I am pleased to announce this year's Modern Dux award and especially pleased to see it go to someone who has shown herself to be a selfless and untiring worker of exemplary character and a great scholar as well," he said. That was enough to make me blush uncontrollably, especially at the mention of that embarrassing word *scholar*.

I was very pleased to escape off the stage, especially as my uniform has become quite scruffy and a little short for me over this past year. It wasn't worth buying a new one for the short time I had left at school.

Over my time at the academy, I have won forty-one prizes—not all of them firsts and not all of them in academic subjects. For instance, I got a third in art in my first year and a third in physical education in my second year. It might sound like vanity to count them all up, but I have a fascination with details. I like to get it exactly right. That has helped me enormously in my studies where accuracy is very important.

Now all the girls, including myself, are considering our future. This is the most difficult time of my life so far, other than the eye glasses issue, of course. Many of the academy girls are leaving to train for a profession in Glasgow or Edinburgh, something their mothers never dreamed of doing. But I am from a farm, and I feel a certain responsibility to return and help out, at least over the busy summer season. The thought of Father managing on his own without our help disturbs me. Both Alison and Margaret are working and so are unavailable to help. Worst of all, it is now wartime, so Father cannot find farm labour in the village. All the young men are away fighting.

This is the first time I have even thought about the war. In the academy, our lives have revolved around our study and school life. The war has seemed light-years away from us. But now, as I leave school, it is becoming a reality. So I think I must do my duty, despite my eagerness to pursue life and all its possibilities outside the village. It is hard for young people, and I am now eighteen, to put their lives on hold because of what is happening so far away from home.

Training Ground

Diary of Jane Haining

August, 1915

I think my time at the farm is nearly up. I am glad I came home to help out after school finished, but my whole heart is hankering for something different to this. As soon as the busy summer period is over, I want to do a training course, I think, in business studies. I have been advised that such a course will offer me good opportunities of work in Glasgow or perhaps Edinburgh, but I would much rather it was Glasgow, as it is not too far from home.

Father has said I should move on, follow my heart's desire, and he will be proud of me whatever I do. Alison has said she may be able to help out as needed on the farm, and in any case, I may have time off from my studies next summer to come home and help as well.

So the decision has been made, and I am taking the big step of applying for a business course at Glasgow Athenaeum. Young women in my generation need to think about their futures and become qualified and employable. The world is changing. We have a war going on, and many young men are being lost at the front. We can no longer rely on finding a suitable husband who will support us for the rest of our lives. And I do not want to be in a position to have to accept an unsuitable husband! We must be independent in a way my mother's generation would never have dreamed of being.

April, 1917

I have been in Glasgow for twenty months now. I am so excited! I have finally been accepted for my first permanent position. Not that it is the best position in the world, but it is a huge step up for a Dunscore farm girl.

I completed eighteen months at the Athenaeum and then with fear and trepidation looked around for a job that would suit me. I took a temporary post in an office to gain a little experience, but now my career seems to be established with a position of clerical assistant for the thread manufacturer J&P Coats in Paisley. This is a big company, and I think, with hard work, I will find opportunity to move into a more responsible position over time. It is not too far from my rooms in Pollokshields, only seven miles, which I can travel by train without a problem.

To be honest, I haven't been back to visit the farm, except for Father's birthday and several other weekends, and I haven't missed it. I'm twenty years old now, and it is time for me to make my own life here in this city.

Changes are afoot at home in Dunscore. Our cousin Margaret, who has been helping run the house for Father is getting married and will leave shortly. My sister Alison has offered to come home and take over. I'm not sure how long that will last, as she also has a sweetheart, and I think wedding bells are in the offing there too. As for me, no such things have entered my head. I am still working to achieve my goals in life, and I am seeking the Lord's guidance on this.

I have found a lovely church to attend, one of the mainstays of my life. Queens Park West offers strong Biblical teaching and traditional, awe-inspiring worship, which sometimes moves me to tears. I have started teaching Sunday school at the church and have loved being able to impart to the children some of the things the Lord has taught me over the past few years.

My heart goes out to children whose fathers are away at war or have been lost in the fighting and others who live a little distance from Queens Park in the poorer suburbs and obviously don't have enough to eat or enough love at home. Life is hard for so many children, and they can so easily turn to vices such as alcohol, gambling, or stealing as they become older. I like working with those just getting to that point because their needs seem to be the most urgent.

Although I love my position at J&P Coats, and I feel I'm doing well there, the highlight of my week is Saturday, when I get a group of my Sunday school pupils together and we head off to the park, or into town to have some fun. The children always have questions for me—sometimes about how to deal with a troublesome sister or brother, sometimes about what is wrong with a glass of beer now and then, as all the children they know sample alcohol from a very early age. But sometimes questions are on more spiritual matters.

Jessie* asked me recently, "When God is talking to you, how do you know it's Him and not just a voice in your head?"

Of course it takes a child to ask the almost unanswerable questions. They are so perceptive. "In the Bible it says God's children know His voice, just like sheep know the voice of their shepherd," I replied.

"But how do you know it's Him and not someone pretending to be Him," she persisted.

"Well, as you read your Bible and pray regularly, you grow closer to God. You begin to know some of His character, and you will know if that voice is telling you something God wouldn't say," I answered, hoping this answer would satisfy her. It did, for the moment at least.

For the younger ones, like nine-year-old Nan Potter, the biggest treat of the outing is the City Bakery cream buns I buy for them before we head back to the church! She always has a huge grin on her face when she sees me bring out the large paper bag of buns. Today, Nan got two buns, as there was one left over, and her smile was twice as broad!

July, 1922

I'm afraid I have not made any entries recently in my diary, but that is because things have been going along smoothly, and I really have not had much to add.

However, a number of changes have now taken place—some good and some rather difficult and confusing.

The good things first, perhaps. I have been promoted to become private secretary to Mr. Peacock, my employer at J&P Coats. He says I am very competent, and I must confess I do enjoy having everything in order and supporting the management of the company in this way.

"We can't do without you, Jane," he said. "This company is becoming more and more dependent on your efficiency, and I must confess I can't imagine it without you."

Another interesting detail of my life is that I have decided to volunteer for the Band of Hope movement that has started up in Glasgow. It has been a natural progression from my work with my Sunday school pupils. We need to reach not just those who come to Sunday school, but also their friends whose influence will otherwise only distract them from the truth and lead them away from the Lord.

So I attend the meetings every Friday night in a local hall as a helper. It has fallen to me to organise skits and activities once a month, and I'm grateful for the opportunities I had at my church in Dunscore to take part in Christmas plays and other performances. Now I need only think back to the things we did there to come up with ideas.

One of the main teachings of Band of Hope is temperance, and I'm passionate about this. But sometimes I lose heart when I find out some of the older boys are coming along to Band of Hope, singing the songs, and joining in with a will but going out and failing to live these ideals out in their everyday lives. This work calls for a faith that sometimes I struggle to conjure up!

Another activity I think I will become involved in, in a service role at least, is the Congregational Mission in Cumberland Street. I'm beginning to see that there is a responsibility for those who have received the truth of the message of the cross to share it with others. For me, to talk to people about my faith is the most daunting thing in the world. I would feel I was flaunting my faith in a most unseemly way. I prefer to let my service speak for itself and trust the Lord to do the actual speaking for me!

A couple of challenges have come my way in the past few months. I am now the secretary of the Sunday school, and I have taken the step of establishing a missions library at the church. This latter has been inspired by my newfound realisation that we must spread the Word to all the world, but also on the prompting of my Canadian cousin, Margaret Coltart, who visited several months ago. We sat down together, and she shared her experiences as a missionary in India, and something inside me responded. I wonder…I wonder if I could ever do what she is doing?

Later

Now for two other events, one confusing and one sad. Father got remarried in January to a neighbour, Robertina Maxwell. While I was very happy for him to find someone, and I knew he was always very lonely there on the farm, his new wife was much younger than him, and I didn't know how I felt about that. Inside, something was saying no one can, or should, replace my mother, but I've never expressed that selfish thought aloud.

Then Father became very ill and died, just one month ago. It was so sudden that we girls didn't have time to get home to see him before his death. That leaves me with the strangest feeling. I think it is what they call unresolved grief. I didn't get to say good-bye.

The whole village attended the funeral, as well as countless relatives. Father was active in local council affairs as well as being an elder at Craig Church, so it was appropriate for him to be farewelled in style. But for me, it is a very private grief.

I feel sorry for Robertina, who is pregnant and now a widow as well. She has returned to her father's farm, as her father is alone, has bad rheumatism, and needs her help.

Our farm is to be sold. It means I now have nowhere to call home. I feel I've been cut adrift, and I'm very thankful that my sister, Margaret, is coming to work in Glasgow, as we can support each other over the next few years.

Diary, I don't want to write any more about this situation. I know I will recover my composure and reinvest myself in my work and other activities that are so dear to my heart. I also know that God is with me at this time of sadness, and I can only think He must have a good purpose in releasing me from these family and farm responsibilities.

August, 1927

I have just heard something that might change my whole life. Diary, you will be the first to hear about it, well before anyone else, because it is a great shock to me, and I am still not sure what it all means.

Last night I attended a talk in Queens Park West Church with a good friend. She suggested we go along, and I went only to accompany her and because I didn't want the church to put on a poor showing for a visiting speaker.

I needn't have worried. The hall was full. The speaker was Reverend Dr. George Mackenzie, and he was speaking about missionary work among the Jews of Central and Eastern Europe. To be truthful, I didn't even know these people existed and certainly had no idea that their needs were so great.

He spoke of the discrimination they suffer, things that horrified me and stirred an anger in me of which I didn't know I was capable. I don't usually react like that.

Many things shocked me. It shocked me that many Jews had been murdered in Hungary's capital, Budapest, for no other reason than that they were Jews, after the Communist uprising was put down there in 1920. They were being targeted because some Jews had supported the Communists.

When I heard that only 20 percent of Jews are allowed to go to university there, I thought of my own freedom to pursue a university education here in Scotland, even though I am a woman.

There are countless other ways their lives are being made difficult. From what he said, it sounds like it is a very dangerous thing to be a Jew in Central and Eastern Europe.

A scripture came to my mind as I listened: Jeremiah 31:2(3) - 3(4) "...I love you with an everlasting love; this is why in my grace

I draw you to me. Once again, I will build you; you will be rebuilt, virgin of Isra'el."

This is the Lord speaking to these same people. How can anyone dare to hate the very people that God loves, and is going to continue to love forever? Those were the questions that burned within me.

In a funny way, I felt last night as though the Lord was also drawing me to Him and to His people. I was so shaken I couldn't think of any question to ask the speaker, although there were lots of questions from other people. As we left the hall, I turned to my friend and found myself saying to her, "I have found my life's work!"

"What do you mean?" she responded.

Stunned by what I'd just said, I hesitated and then answered, "I don't really know. This lecture has really affected me. I don't think I can dismiss what I heard tonight."

My own pronouncement certainly shocked me more than her. Whatever does it mean? We walked to my rooms and shared a cup of tea and some ginger biscuits I'd baked earlier in the day and chatted about our jobs and daily lives. Nothing more was said about the evening speaker.

July, 1931

Things are moving very fast now, so I must put pen to paper once more. Eighteen months ago I decided I had to do something about the talk I had heard about the Jews of Eastern Europe. I just couldn't forget it. In our church notices there was mention made of a meeting of the Jewish Mission Committee of the Church of Scotland, so I decided to attend.

I was surprised to find the same Dr. MacKenzie there, now the convenor of the committee. I told him about the impact his talk in 1927 had had on me, and he was genuinely interested. I said I wanted to serve in some way but was unsure of how God was leading me on this. He suggested I wait for confirmation of the direction I should take.

But waiting is not one of my strong points. Not that I'm impulsive, but if there is action to be taken, I always want to attend to it as soon as possible. So I did. I told Mr. Peacock I was resigning! He was quite upset and did all he could to dissuade me. Several months later, he fell ill with an infection that he couldn't throw off, and I found myself managing his work as well as my own for the next five months until he was well enough to come back to work. I realised then how much he had come to rely on my secretarial and managerial skills. So when I broached the subject of leaving again and saw the look of mild panic on his face, I agreed to wait another year. That would give him time to train up someone else for the post.

When I told my friends of my decision, I can say almost 100 percent of them were horrified that I, of all people, would do something so radical! They wondered what I would do—actually, I was wondering that secretly myself. But I showed them a strong and resolute front.

The next few months were a time of soul searching. How was I to prepare myself for this call of the Lord, which I still didn't understand? I discussed my future with some trusted church friends, and the general consensus was that I should follow my heart's desire. As I have always wanted to have charge of a girls' home, something like the Bridge of Weir Home I have heard of near Glasgow, I decided to study for a diploma at the Domestic Sciences College in Glasgow.

So here I am, back at school and undertaking a housekeeper's certificate course to ensure I have all the qualifications I need if in fact my calling is to work in a girls' home. I'm very glad I have lived frugally while working in Paisley as, without my savings, this course of study would not have been possible for me. It is difficult to live on savings alone, but I believe I have enough so long as there is a paying job in the not too distant future for me.

I have decided to keep up my evening German lessons. I have not lost my love of languages, and it is important to keep using the skills one already has. My German class is quite small, so it is an excellent opportunity for me to improve my pronunciation.

My tutor says I'm fast becoming fluent.

My life must not be dominated completely by my straightened financial situation!

February, 1932

Diary, you will be flabbergasted by this entry. You know I'm not one to exaggerate or even to draw attention to myself and what I do, but this is something to take notice of.

I am off to Budapest in less than four months to take up the position of matron in the Church of Scotland's Scottish Mission to Budapest Girls' Home.

How did this all happen? I finished my domestic science course, passing with distinction, and had to find work to tide me over while I found my life's work. It is very hard to find your life's work if you don't know where to search! So I took a temporary office job in Glasgow and then found a job as matron in a radium institute in Manchester. That, at least, would give me experience in the field I believe God wants me to work in.

Manchester is farther away from home than I have been before, and I have sorely missed my friends. One lovely saint from Queens Park Church, Miss Munro (she likes to be called Miss Munro, so funnily enough I never found out her first name!), has kept me informed of Glasgow happenings by sending me the Church of Scotland *Life and Works* magazine every month. How typical of her. She is a very faithful servant of the Lord.

It was in this magazine that I found the advertisement about the matron's position in Budapest. Not only did I have the right qualifications, including my domestic sciences diploma, an ability in German, and basic musical skills, but it was also a position working among the Jews.

The girls' home caters to Jews and Gentiles. In these uncertain times in Budapest, many Jewish families are sending their girls to board there. I'm told the school has a very high academic standard, something the Jewish parents value enormously. They are apparently unconcerned that the school and home is Christian, with the declared purpose of converting any who attend to Christianity. I will have to see exactly what that means in practice, as I believe we are all equal, and equally loved by God, and the Jewish children must not be required to lose their Jewishness in order to gain our Lord.

So I applied at once, and it just flowed on from there. I found myself in front of the selection committee, and the next thing I knew, I heard the words, "I think we need to go no further in looking for the right candidate, Miss Haining."

I was selected for the position. I am more than excited about this.

The one concern they had was that I would have the ability to learn Hungarian, which is a difficult language. The secretary for the

Overseas Department of the Church of Scotland, Reverend Dr. MacDonald Webster, consulted Mr. Peacock at J&P Coats, who assured him I was more than able in this regard. I do hope I do not disappoint him in this.

My next step will be a period of training at St. Colm's Women's Ministry College in Edinburgh. This college trains Church of Scotland missionaries. I still can't believe that I am about to train to become a missionary. But of course, I will not be like the missionaries one thinks of who travel around preaching and teaching from the Bible among pagan tribes in distant lands. My service will be of a much humbler kind and really not that much different from what I am now doing in Manchester.

PART THREE: BUDAPEST

My Life's Work

Diary of Jane Haining

September, 1932

Where can I start? I'm finally here in Budapest, the matron of the girls' home for the Scottish Mission. I can still scarcely believe it.

The past few months have gone by so quickly, and I have had to make radical changes both in the way I think and in the way I do things, but I will never make changes in the most important thing, my dependence on the Lord for all I need.

I completed my training at St. Colm's Women's Missionary College in Edinburgh, where I met many inspiring people who were training for mission fields all over the world. My observations of these people confirmed my thoughts that I was not cut out to be a missionary of that stature, but would simply serve the Lord in whatever He opened up to me. The high-profile work of evangelism was not for me.

I had a lovely dedication service in June at Edinburgh's St. Stephen's Church with the convenor of the Jewish Mission Committee and minister of the church, Dr. T. B. Stewart Thompson, officiating. He led the congregation in committing me to God's grace, and I know I'm going to need a lot of that here as I struggle with a few of the more unruly children.

I thoroughly enjoyed the trip by train to Budapest. It was my first time outside England and Scotland, so I had a lot to learn and take in. Fortunately I had had a lot of advice about the journey, and everything went exactly as planned. How glad I was that I had studied languages and was prepared for another culture where not everyone spoke English. I think I may have brought a little too much luggage—I will reduce that on further trips—but I did want to bring as much as I could, especially photos of my family and also a number of gifts given to me before I left, some of which I will pass on to the girls in the home. However, I find that Budapest has everything you could want, so I needn't have worried so much when packing.

I was met at the station by a tallish lady, Margit Prém, who has been the acting matron of the girls' home as well as the headmistress of the mission's Higher School. I was amazed she had found time to come down to the train station to give me a personal welcome despite her enormous work load. I took an immediate liking to this Miss Prém with her matter-of-fact manner.

"Hello," she said, in good but clipped English. "You must be our new matron. How lovely of you to come from so far away to work in our small school. I will make sure you have all you need for your work and will organise people to show you around. Come this way, please."

We managed to manhandle my suitcases into a taxi and headed straight for the school and girls' home, which are in the same building on Vörösmarty utca (*utca* means street), very close to the centre of town. I immediately fell in love with this grandiose building with its magnificent winding staircase and balconied upper floors. It reminds me a lot of Moat House in Dumfries. The girls' home is on the fourth floor overlooking a small courtyard, which is encircled by the building. We have easy access to the chapel, which is connected to the school by a small door on the ground floor.

I had one of the most welcome cups of tea I have ever had, and then met Dr. William Beveridge, the missionary in charge, who had resigned from the position but waited here in Budapest until I came. How considerate that was of him.

My first few days were spent looking around Budapest, guided by various people at the mission. What a beautiful city! In some ways, it reminds me of Glasgow with its old but magnificent buildings in many different architectural styles, which tell the history of the city. Not wanting to waste a moment of my time, I noted sites that would be good to show my future charges. There is just so much here for them to see, and, I'm told, many children don't get the opportunity to go anywhere outside the Jewish Quarter (their parents are too busy). We will soon change that.

Then I found myself on an old bus with a dozen girls, mostly Jewish, headed for a rented house on the shores of Lake Balaton, a popular holiday spot not far from Budapest, where we were to spend two months of the summer vacation. This was my first real introduction to the children I would be looking after and a chance for me to learn about them and how they thought and behaved.

I was in for some surprises. Of course they are like all six-to-fourteen-year-olds in that they want to have fun and desperately need to be loved but also need a firm hand at times. I found them quite unlike their Scottish counterparts, however, in that most of the girls seemed quite precocious, compared to the children I taught in Sunday school in Scotland anyway. They are very intelligent and very sociable once they trust you, and I can see I will have to have my wits about me to keep up with them. I immediately fell in love with two young girls, Katinka* and Magdalena*, both Jewesses who obviously had had no mother to hug them every morning and no training in how to keep themselves and their surroundings tidy.

51

"But you must put your clothes away in your locker every night before you get into bed, Katinka," I would say, as I found another pile of clothes under her bed.

This would be met by a cheeky grin and a nod of agreement. I would go away, satisfied that my request had been understood and would be acted upon, only to find the next night her towel and face cloth trying to find their own way back along the corridor from the bathroom to her bedroom.

With the help of two other staff—I needed their help, as my three or four words in Hungarian weren't enough to get by on— we had a great time, spending the mornings roaming around the lake shore in search of all sorts of wonderful creatures and racing to see who could be first to get into the lake to cool off in the humid afternoons. I made a mental note to find some better clothes for some of the girls, who looked like they had been dressed by the rag lady.

The girls delighted in teaching me Hungarian words, some of which I later found I should not repeat! They teased me unceasingly about my strong Scottish accent, and I would hear them mimicking me in their bedroom after lights out.

"The puir bairns 'r tired." I could hear their suppressed giggles. "I dinna ken what I'd do without ye lassie." More giggles followed.

But it was all in the best humour, and we all had a good laugh. I think my first encounter with my Hungarian charges has been a great success, and I am now really looking forward to the new school term and meeting the others as they arrive at the home this weekend.

December, 1932

I have been matron for four months now and am feeling much more secure in my job. I am being paid 100 pounds per annum and receive full board, including laundry, with a fully furnished and comfortable room.

My first goal has been to begin lessons in Hungarian, the language that all the children speak. For the Christian girls, this is their mother tongue and even for most of the Jewesses, as many speak no Hebrew and only a smattering of Yiddish at home. It seems many of them have lost part of their identity as Jews in that their families have been so torn apart by multiple divorces and remarriages. It also seems the Jewish community here would like to feel they are assimilated, probably to keep a low profile in the community after all the troubles that followed the unfortunate uprising in 1919 by the Communists. They say many Jews were murdered on the streets after that, for no reason other than their Jewishness.

I have already seen the damage done by the discriminatory laws that followed in 1920 that allowed only 20 percent of Jews to go on to higher education. I'm told that many Jews have had to go abroad to go to university, and others have changed their religion to Christianity in order to access higher education. This produces a great dilemma.

Only a few months ago, I would have thought that that might have been a good outcome to a bad event. After all, are we not here to do exactly that, convert the Jewish population? But now, even in this short time, I am seeing things differently. I have got to know these Jewish families and their girls and am fast becoming very attached to them.

Now, as I pick up my Bible, I'm suddenly seeing scriptures in it that have been there all the time but are now speaking clearly to me of God's peculiar love for these people. The Bible makes clear that God actually loved the Jews as Jews and didn't ever ask them to change their identity.

The Jewish Mission Committee states that we are to bring the gospel of Christ to Budapest and to the Jews living here as a love offering, but also that all Jewish children staying in the girls' home must receive tuition in their faith from Jewish teachers each week. So clearly, the mission also values their culture and beliefs highly.

Exactly what that means for me I have yet to find out. What I do know is that my spirit registers a sadness each time I hear of one of these dear souls feeling they have to give up their own identity and put on ours in order to get on in life and get an education in this country. I am as determined as I was the day I arrived to see the gospel spread to the Jews, but this is not the way to do it!

Fortunately, things have eased up a little, and now the rules have changed so that a quota system exists along social lines for entry into university. This still discriminates against Jews but in a different way. So now I have the practical problem of how to persuade the Jewish girls in the home that, although the laws of the land say otherwise, they are just as important and have as bright a future as everyone else. Hopefully things will improve further and this will not be a long-term problem.

Now, back to the other practical issue—the need to be able to talk fluently to these girls. So far, I have been using German, and relying on the Jewesses' limited Yiddish, which is very like German, to understand me, but I'm glad to say I now have a tutor to help me improve my Hungarian. Edith Roda, head of the elementary school, has offered to be my tutor, and I am really grateful for this. I am thoroughly enjoying my lessons and am making surprisingly fast progress. One should not allow oneself to become downhearted by any comments or warnings such as I received from a few concerned friends before coming here. "Hungarian is a very hard language to learn. It will be a long time before you can really have a conversation with your charges," they told me. Others had assured me if anyone was capable of picking up this language quickly, it was me. I preferred to listen to this advice.

My weekly schedule is very full. We had only thirty boarders at the mission when I arrived, but already numbers are increasing. My responsibilities include providing clean and healthy boarding facilities for the girls, along with healthy meals and plenty of exercise and activities to keep them busy in their free time.

But in reality, it is far more than that. I endeavour to create a home away from home for these girls, many of whom are unwanted and some even abandoned. It is a challenging job to become mother to about thirty girls all at once. I have to be very careful to be fair to all and have no favourites. For instance, when mothers send along sweets or cakes for their children, as quite often happens in the more stable families, I take the gifts and distribute them to all the children after school as a treat for all so that the little ones who do not have a caring mother to send them things do not feel left out.

But alongside that, there are times when one child does need a special hug and extra attention, and I am becoming more adept each day in spotting that child in the crowd. I think I understand how they feel, especially the little new girls, as I remember back to my days at Dumfries Academy and how homesick I was at first.

What must flow through everything I do with the girls is the love of the Lord for them. If these girls don't feel loved by me, how can they ever find the One who loves them most?

I am also responsible for their spiritual education to some extent. As a mission, we provide lessons on religion in the school, as all schools must do by law in Hungary, but I must also take every opportunity to model what a happy Christian family is like.

This means saying grace before meals—that confuses some of the younger Jewish girls, as at home they say it after meals—and bedtime prayers. I'm helped in the latter by other staff members who each take turns in the dormitories to read a scripture and pray with the girls.

Of course on Sundays, we get the girls dressed up in their best clothes and attend a morning church meeting, either in the adjacent church or at the home if there is no service in the church that day. Immediately afterwards, we hold our Sunday school classes, in which the girls learn in small groups about the Bible. On Sunday evenings, we also have our own devotion time, and I try to encourage the girls to take turns to present a small scripture and talk about what it means to them.

I have started teaching the girls the Lord's Prayer. We say it one night in English, the next in German, and the third night in Hungarian, which is also good practice for me. I am concerned at how little of the scriptures some of the girls know by heart. I think I will make this a focus for a while.

As well as the care of the children, I am also responsible for hosting any visiting guests, which means making sure meals are catered and accommodation provided somewhere in the community for them. Because this mission is very active, I am expecting many visitors and can see this will take up whatever time is left in my schedule.

But I must be mindful always to spend my morning and evening quiet times with the Lord, even if it is at three in the morning! That is where I have always got my strength from, and something tells me this position is going to require more strength than I can produce by myself.

August, 1934

Another glorious summer at Lake Balaton. I have little to report of the past year and a half, which perhaps is a good thing. The work has progressed very well with the number of boarders increasing a little each year.

This year the school rented a house by the lake, which was not close to any Hungarian Reformed Church, so I found myself not only matron and mother but pastor also, taking worship services each Sunday in the house. It has proved a wonderful opportunity for the girls to ask questions about religion, and some have been very interested. Maria*, in particular, listened very attentively to the simple sermons I preached and has asked some interesting questions about the doctrine of original sin and the meaning of repentance. I believe some seeds have been sown there.

We have had the usual cases of homesickness, especially with the youngest newcomers, but these all resolved themselves quickly as soon as I enlisted the help of older girls to take new ones under their wings. Several of the older girls have taken to this role with great enthusiasm, reminding me of my days at Dumfries Academy, where I liked nothing better than to help a new student adjust to the school. Nadia*, in particular, loves this role and in April volunteered to sleep in the junior dormitory with a group of new girls until they were well settled in. There are two dormitories with up to twenty-six girls in the junior one and twenty in the senior.

I am certainly learning how much some of these girls need mothering. I have now taken to collecting their school books from their teachers each day and handing them out for evening study periods. That way, the excuse that they forgot to bring their book upstairs after class is to no avail. Of course, I also have to make

57

sure each girl has her books ready for school each morning, which may seem bothersome but is actually the easiest way to ensure all arrive at the classroom properly equipped for their day of study.

One special incident stands out from the past year, so I should include it here in my diary. Our little Gitta* told me her dream was to become a teacher one day, like Aunty Sophie Victor. This presented a big problem because Gitta didn't know she had been handed over by her Jewish parents to be adopted by a Christian couple. She had no idea she was Jewish as more and more Jewish families had been choosing to live as non-Jews, bringing their children up in complete ignorance of their origins to try and escape the harsh restrictions on their futures. Gitta was too young when handed over to the Christian couple to understand any of that. But escaping the consequences of being Jewish was, and is, actually a futile hope. Her chances of fulfilling her dreams in adulthood are very likely to be hindered by her true identity. Even though she will be adopted into a Christian family, she will in the future find all sorts of restrictions on her life because of her Jewish heritage.

My heart wept for her as she told me of all her dreams for her future, her face shining with anticipation. She had to be told the truth. I gathered her up on my knee and explained to her as gently as I could her true origins.

"You know, Gitta, there are some things in our lives that we don't understand," I began. "You have a lovely mama and papa who love you very much, but did you know you are a special little girl and have another mama as well? She also loves you very much. You know how Katinka and Magdalena are special little girls because they are Jewesses? Well your other mama is also a Jewess just like them, and that means you are too. So when the rabbi comes to talk to all the Jewish children here, that means you can go along with them too, if you wish. But it also means when you grow up all the rules for Jews are for you too."

Of course it was a harsh reality for a young child to face. I held her for a long time in silence before she slipped off my knee and disappeared into the dormitory.

I think the next step for me will be to arrange for little Gitta to meet her real mother, who has kept in contact with the school, thankfully. Perhaps I can arrange a special present to be sent from her birth mother. How harsh this world is for some! At least I know what it feels like to be motherless from a young age, but the circumstances for these children are harsher than for most, with unemployment and family breakdown endemic here.

February, 1937

Again, a big gap since I last wrote here, but for the same reason. Things are going very well with my job, although I have to admit I have become very tired sometimes.

We have had bouts of influenza, and over the past Christmas holiday, we had an epidemic of scarlet fever. I had some girls so sick that I was very concerned about them. I took several to sleep in my room overnight to keep an eye on them. Fever can be so dangerous in a small child.

Now our governess, who conducts the girls' evening studies, has been taken ill, and I have had to find a substitute for her until she is well again. I'm greatly relieved that there are several women who are kind enough to volunteer their services in such emergencies, but of course they can never achieve what Miss Toth does with her even measure of jocularity and strict discipline.

The weather isn't helping either. It has been colder than I have known it in Hungary, with snow falling for days on end. The city is certainly beautiful under its layer of snow, but it means I can't take the girls out on their usual excursions. I try to get them out for an hour at least every day after school. Their favourite destination is a local pond where they can ice skate. We are all waiting impatiently for spring to arrive.

Something happened about eighteen months ago that I can't dismiss from my mind, so, diary, you will have to bear with me unloading it here. I have never taken an interest in politics, but this one event strikes me with foreboding.

I hadn't taken any notice of the rise to power of Adolf Hitler in Germany at the end of January, 1933. I was too busy getting my new life sorted out here in Budapest. But recently, there has been talk around the town, and I simply can't avoid it, that the actions of this leader do not bode well for the Jewish people anywhere— not just in Germany, but here too! What have upset people are the new laws they call the Nuremburg Laws that were passed in Germany in the autumn of 1935 (September, I think). These laws not only brought back military service in Germany but also introduced new racial laws with Jews as the obvious target.

At his Nazi Party conference in Nuremburg, Hitler introduced laws forbidding Jews from marrying or having extramarital sex with what he calls Aryans. (That is us, I think. Apparently we are superior in some way.) Surely that is taking government too far—in fact, right into people's bedrooms! Other restrictions on Jews employing young Aryan women in their homes were also introduced.

While I'm told the reason for these laws is the rising level of unrest and violence against the Jews in Germany and other places, it defies logic to see how such laws can possibly be the solution.

I have heard that these laws are based on excellent, in fact leading, scientific thought in the study of eugenics. The name Sir Francis Galton, cousin of the man who tells us we have descended from monkeys, Charles Darwin, is bandied around in connection to these eugenics theories. I would not ever presume to understand these things, but I can see with my own eyes that these theories, which say some races are superior to others, cannot be correct. The Jewish race is not an inferior race in any way. My Jewish girls are as intelligent and bright as any I have ever met.

Perhaps I am making too much of this incident and things will stabilize. Nevertheless, I do worry about the futures my girls have to look forward to, and I will do my very best to make their present situation as loving and secure as I can.

The Bible tells us not to dwell on the bad but remind ourselves of the good and of the Lord's blessings in our lives. There is a scripture I need to pin up on my wall. It is Philippians 4:8, "In conclusion, brothers, focus your thoughts on what is true, noble, righteous, pure, lovable, or admirable, on some virtue or on something praiseworthy."

So I will list some of the good things happening here at the Scottish Mission to bring some light into the lives of our girls and to further the cause of the mission. We regularly hold special events such as the Sunshine Feasts, during which we put on plays, have lots of games, a special afternoon tea, and even sometimes give out small gifts to each girl; our Christmas Eve parties (always hugely successful with the girls and their parents); and of course birthday parties for each girl.

I'm pleased to say that about fifty girls from the school also attend the school's Girl Scout unit, which takes them on weekend camps and gives godly input into their lives as well. I am not in charge of this but am often called upon to help with catering for their special events.

Other good things that have happened in the past couple of years are the arrival of Reverend George A. F. Knight from Scotland in 1935 to take over as the mission director and my furlough in Scotland in 1935. I am also looking forward to my trip to Switzerland with my sister Margaret in our spring break coming up later this year.

Reverend Knight has been a godsend. He amazed us all with his fluent Hungarian on his first day here and has been a strong influence in the war against rising anti-Semitism here and abroad—anywhere Hungarian is spoken. I have listened to him speaking to groups in the city on this subject and am aware that in some quarters, what he has to say has not been well received.

My furlough for two months meant that I missed out on going to Lake Balaton. Instead, I returned to Scotland to see my family and my friends in Glasgow. It was lovely to worship once again in the Queens Park West Church. I decided not to talk to groups about the work of the mission while there, and I think that was a good decision, as I was very tired and sorely needed the break. I often work seven days a week, so the time was very precious. In any case, there are others who would do a much better job than me in publicising the work.

A development that has delighted me is the recent formation of a Former Pupils' Club. It is going to be absolutely strategic in solving one major problem we have here at the mission. According to Hungarian law, no one under the age of eighteen may change their faith. While we don't push for conversions— quite the reverse—we still want to keep in contact with those among our Jewish pupils who show an interest in the Bible and Christian teachings. However, we have been losing contact with the girls after they leave school at either fourteen or fifteen years old. Many times, the school has been their home—for some, their only home.

We need to have ongoing input, and this club will provide that. It has already shown signs of being very successful with good attendances and good comments. The girls themselves want to keep in contact with each other, and I think they may well do so for the rest of their lives. I personally want to be part of that too!

Ripples on the Water

Diary of Jane Haining

December, 1937

Well, what a year this has been! We, that is, the Scottish Mission to Budapest, are being inundated with requests for help from all quarters.

I look out my window when I have a free moment during the day and see queues of people waiting outside on the pavement to see Reverend Knight or one of the other leaders of the mission. It is the most deplorable sight—their faces carry a hopelessness I don't think I have seen before. They are refugees, Jews who have fled Poland, Austria, and Germany mainly because of the harsh, repressive laws being introduced everywhere where that man Hitler holds influence. I cannot understand how he has gained such power over the minds of the German people and their neighbours.

The refugees are seeking the most basic of help—food, clothing, a safe place to live. They get no help whatsoever from the Hungarian government as they are not citizens. In fact, I'm not sure how they have managed to get to Hungary at all. I think most do not have the correct papers to travel, so I imagine they have been smuggled across the borders.

I am not sure what to make of all this. I know Reverend Knight is working night and day to help these people, but more just keep coming. He has requested money from the Jewish Mission Committee in Scotland to help some of the neediest, and some money has been sent.

I have had some Jewish parents come to me and ask if it is safe for them to remain in Hungary! More Jews are asking to enrol their children at the school, I think, because this is a Christian school, and they see it as a safe haven where they know they will be treated as equals. There seems to be a sense of unease among the Budapest Jewish population, possibly the result of these other Jews arriving with their nightmare stories of persecution, beatings in the streets, and loss of employment for seemingly no reason.

But it is not so here. There are restrictions, but Jews can still work and still go about the city unharmed, as far as I am aware. In fact, that is why the other Jews are coming to Hungary.

Meanwhile, my job is to make sure my girls are safe and happy in the home and to shield them from the troubles that seem to be growing in number out there in the world. Recently, I took all of them—from the youngest to the oldest—for a night out to see the lights that now illuminate the Chain Bridge, which spans the River Duna (Danube). It was a glorious sight—quite spectacular! The lights have been erected in preparation for the visit of Italian king Victor Emmanual III and Austrian Chancellor Edler von Schuschnigg. The younger girls are now asking that we decorate the mission with lights for our Christmas festivities. I will look into what we can do, but I think it is unlikely that we are going to match the Chain Bridge display.

Last week, one of the younger girls gave me a bookmark, quite out of the blue.

"This is for you, Miss Haining," she said, looking up anxiously into my face. "I did it myself. Do you like it?"

She had written on it a scripture, which she must have known was one of my favourites: "Be not afraid, only believe" (Mark 5:36).[1]

It was such a sweet gesture, especially coming from one who has taken some time to settle in here and has been very slow to allow me to put my arm around her to give her a cuddle. She has lost her father (he has had to move to another country to find work and is not able to come home), and her mother now has to go out to work six days a week in a factory to support her five children. I have made an arrangement with this family to take little Dorika* at a very reduced boarding fee, as they are simply unable to survive in their present circumstances. I am keeping this bookmark in my Bible.

I have been very remiss in my correspondence with the folks at home recently. No doubt they wonder how I am faring, but I think they know me well enough to expect that I am riding all the storms of the current situation well. In fact I am enjoying the mounting challenges as the economy tightens, and the pengo[2] has to be made to stretch further. My administrative skills come to the fore here, and I am thankful to God for my training at J&P Coats in making the books balance.

Next week, I will have to start searching for little presents for each of the girls, and for the staff too, to hand out at our Christmas Eve party. The children just love getting presents, and I try to make sure each one has personal meaning for the recipient. For the staff, I sometimes get joke presents. This time, I think I will get a feather duster for one of our cleaning staff and write a funny comment on it as dusting is the job she hates most. There are more than forty staff members in all, including teachers, so shopping for presents is not a small job.

June, 1938

This year has started with some very unsettling events, which I had hoped would not affect Hungary and especially not the already traumatised Jewish people of this country.

The first came as a great shock to me. I don't follow political events closely, as I am unable to be of influence and so concentrate on where I can be of influence—with my girls in the home here. But this event, what they call the Anschluss, or annexation of Austria, on March 12, has caught the attention of all.

I was working in my office, updating records, when our assistant pastor at the mission, Reverend Gyula Forgács, came rushing in. "Miss Haining, Miss Haining, have you heard the news?" he spluttered. "I cannot believe this has happened!"

Of course I said I hadn't and was about to go back to my books when he dropped the bombshell about the annexation. I could see how agitated he was, so I immediately made him a cup of tea and sat down with him while he explained the situation to me.

Austria shares a long border with Hungary, so I can understand his concern. However, our lives are not in Hitler's hands but in God's, and I am currently feeling very thankful for that. I am more determined than ever that these young girls in my care will be kept safe and as far away as possible from the troublesome happenings out there. I need to give them as close to a normal home as possible in these abnormal times.

Obviously the new proximity of German influence has affected Hungary for the worse. On May 29, some new laws were passed that have huge ramifications for us at the mission. These laws restrict the number of Jews in any profession to only 20 percent.

As most are aware, the Jews have played a significant role in the business, artistic, and professional life of Budapest. I don't know how they will cope, as many will lose jobs in an already badly depressed economy. Many will no longer be able to afford the fees for our mission school, which is actually the one stable thing in their children's lives.

More and more Jewish families are converting to Christianity in an attempt to avoid the consequences of these Jewish Laws. I understand why they would do this and am grief stricken by their predicament, but I have to ask whether these conversions have any substance in faith! I would dearly love them to have the assurance and peace that I have from that wonderful passage in Romans 8: 31, "If God is for us, who can be against us?" Soon it will be very hard to tell who has, and who has not, made a real decision to follow our Saviour!

I have written a note home to assure my family and friends that the mission is untouched by these political events. Our role here is becoming more important daily. Not only has there been debate on the political front, but also there has been debate for some time now about what to do with the increasing number of Jewish children who discover their Lord and Messiah. There were very few conversions when I first took up the position of matron at the home, but as life becomes more difficult in the world out there, more and more girls are seeking real answers to their deepest questions about their identity and about Jesus.

I am adamant that all I want to do is point these girls to their own Jewish scriptures, where I believe all the answers are to be found. However, problems arise once those answers are found! Some overseeing the mission to the Jews believe these Christian Jews need to assimilate into our Christian churches. Some say they need their own special churches, and others believe they should continue to attend their synagogues, acting as biblical leaven.

From time to time, I am asked for my opinion on this, but I don't have an answer. In fact, it is an issue outside of what I came here to do. But I do see the Former Pupils' Club as one short-term solution. At least they can meet there together and study the Bible without being forced into any of the above camps.

We could discuss and argue forever on this issue, but meanwhile there is work to do. I have taken over the English-speaking Sunday school, despite my already heavy workload. I enjoy so much teaching the young girls about our Lord, and when doing so, I feel I am really at the heart of what the Lord wants me to do here. So it is a joy, rather than a burden.

The winter has again been a long one, and we have had a bad influenza epidemic. At least this time, I have been more prepared for it than in previous years and have converted a spare room into a large sick bay to cope with the girls who need to be in isolation. Our local doctor is very good, coming at very short notice, even during the night, if I feel the need to call him.

It is the thought of two months at Lake Balaton again that is keeping me going. We are taking fifteen girls this time, almost all of whom have lost at least one parent one way or another. Among them will be four Austrian Jews we have taken into the home this year. Their families fled from Austria just before the annexation. They had to come with nothing but the clothes on their backs. I am shocked that the world can show such hatred to these ones. Two of them cry incessantly at night. They need as much love as I and the rest of our staff can give them.

June, 1939

The busier I get, the fewer entries in my diary! But significant events require another entry. Here I am in my forty-third year, and the world seems to be turning upside down. I have barely had time to celebrate my birthday this year, and wouldn't have, if it had not been for the intervention of some of the senior girls at the home. They produced a lovely afternoon tea for me.

Since my last diary entry, a huge amount has happened here in Europe, but my life and work have not changed greatly. In September last year, Germany was given a large chunk of Czechoslovakia, and in March of this year, somehow, the Germans managed to take over the rest of it by diplomacy rather than guns, I'm glad to say. But what they call the Third Reich is busy arming itself, and pity those who stand in its way!

Hungary has passed the second Jewish law, on May 5, this time reducing the percentage of Jews allowed in the professions to only 5 percent. This will seriously affect the large Jewish population of Budapest with huge job losses. Fifteen boarders' families are now reduced to begging for food. We are being very circumspect about collecting fees in these cases, and I know Reverend Knight has managed to get quite a lot of support funding from the Church of Scotland for these families.

I have only just realised another ramification, besides the obvious economic one, of this law. We had been hoping that all those Jews who chose to take the Messiah as their Saviour and be baptised in the name of Jesus, would escape the effects of these Jewish laws, because they now consider themselves Christian. But this law defines a Jew as a person having two or more Jewish grandparents. For the first time, Jews are being defined as a race with no consideration to their religion. There have been many who have converted to avoid these laws, and I understand fully why they should do so, but from now on, any converts will surely be real ones!

In the light of these changes, our new initiative takes on much more importance. The mission has established a training school for young women wanting to find work as domestic servants overseas. I have already given some lectures on British society to prepare those who are able to find work in my home country. Reverend Knight and I both believe the best thing for many Jews in Hungary would be to emigrate to a safer land, preferably well away from continental Europe. We see it as the only solution to the oppressive laws that seem to be spreading so quickly from country to country.

This view is not held widely internationally, or else people do not know what is going on in Europe as we know of few initiatives to help Jews to emigrate at present, except the provision for a small number to go to Palestine. I hope to have the opportunity to share my concerns while in Britain on furlough in just a few weeks' time.

September, 1939

I am still amazed at the news I have to record below in this diary. It was so totally unexpected, and I'm not sure what the future now holds for countless millions of people, but I am convinced my way forward is as clear as the day I first arrived in Budapest.

My furlough in Britain has gone very well. I took Miss Prém with me this time. She has become a very good friend and loves to make speeches. That is very fortunate, as we have received a lot of invitations to speak during our time here, including one to my old Glasgow church, Queens Park West.

We took every opportunity to warn those we spoke to about the worsening situation for the Jews in Europe, but I still wonder sometimes if the message has fallen on deaf ears. Perhaps it was so far outside the experience of most people that they thought we were exaggerating for effect!

At one meeting I said, "The Jews of Europe are in huge danger. They are discriminated against at every level and some are even going missing—unexplained disappearances."

"But surely you are dramatising a situation that is simply the result of the political unrest throughout Europe at present. It is happening to any who are vulnerable in society," announced one stalwart defender of the status quo. "I understand your need to publicise your work. I'm sure the Jews are suffering, but so are the poor in every country in Europe." My heart sank into my boots!

It was so lovely to see my family again after so long, and I made a special effort to visit my half-sister Agnes, whom I have had so little chance to get to know. She is now quite a young lady and is at the stage where she is wondering what to do with her life. It occurred to me that a few months in Budapest with the mission would be a wonderful experience for her, so I invited her to return with us. She was very excited by the idea.

Miss Prém and I then went down to Kent to visit my sister Margaret, and that was when we heard the news. Germany had decided to attack Poland, for some reason, and entirely overwhelmed that nation within days.

To make matters worse, France and England declared war on Germany. With this news, we knew we had to make the greatest haste back to Budapest before European transport became so disrupted that travel would be impossible.

It was now unthinkable that we would take Agnes back to Hungary with us, and I must say she looked most disappointed. But I'm sure she had no idea of the seriousness of the situation. I suggested she could come over for a visit when the situation had settled down a bit, or when this war was over, which of course must be very soon.

Many friends have been trying to persuade me to stay in England, but it is totally unthinkable that I should abandon my post. Not only that, I need to accompany Miss Prém on the return journey. Leaving her to travel back alone at such a time as this is also unthinkable.

So suitcases have been hurriedly packed and tickets bought for the journey. We set out tomorrow, several days before our originally planned departure date.

In the Throes of War

Diary of Jane Haining

October, 1939

I'm now back in Hungary at the girls' home and very glad to be here. It seems we are in the thick of the action at the mission. But first, the journey back here. It contrasts greatly with my other journeys across Europe, showing the huge disruption already caused by this war.

Miss Prém and I boarded our train in London without problem and made it through to Calais in France by ferry, again without problem. That was when the difficulties arose. We had a two-hour wait for our next train but found trains were no longer running according to schedule. In fact, they came when they came, no sooner and no later. Also, the route we had planned had been changed, and so we could no longer get a train from Calais to Paris and then one through to Budapest. Oh no! It took us five changes of train, each with long waits on draughty train station platforms.

At Calais, we had only a four-hour wait. If we had known what was ahead, we would not have complained about that! We squeezed onto the overbooked train and had to stand for much of the journey to Paris.

It seemed that half the French population was shifting house and taking everything with them on the train. I have never seen so many people with so many bags. I even saw one farming family trying to struggle aboard at a small country stop with two chickens, a dog, three or four children, and at least eight bags. I think a lot of these travellers would be hoping to head south, as far away as possible from the threat of a German invasion.

Babies were crying, children were subdued and confused, and their parents generally looked tense and said little. This was certainly no holiday for any of us and a very strange end to my furlough. One of the biggest problems was the lack of sanitary conveniences, and at stations where there were such conveniences, the sheer numbers of people wanting to use them soon rendered them inoperable. I think we British travellers, with our greater modesty, suffered more as a result of this problem than the French, who are in such things, very practical!

We also found it hard to find any food, as the station kiosks were either closed or had run out of food before we arrived. I was very glad of the sandwiches Margaret had made for us before we left. We rationed these, eating only two sandwiches a day, and finding water to drink at taps on some of the stations where we stopped.

One of our two longest stops was at Paris, where we had to spend the night on the platform, sitting on our bags, always hoping the train would turn up soon. To leave the platform could have meant missing the train, so finding a hotel was out of the question. To leave our bags unattended was also out of the question. All platforms were crowded. Rumours were flying around thick and fast that the train services had been completely cancelled, as trains were needed to take soldiers to the front, and that the Germans had bombed the rail line so no trains could get through. There were no official announcements (Miss Prém and I could both speak a little French, and we would have understood any announcement), so all we could do was wait. Fortunately the weather was balmy, as it often is in Paris in September.

The second long stop, and by now we were very tired indeed after three days' travel, was in the middle of nowhere, in a small village near Leoban in Austria. I have no idea why we stopped there. Here again, we had to wait overnight, but this time it was on an unsheltered platform in considerably cooler weather. We both felt somewhat intimidated by the regular passage of German officials of one sort or another across the platform and into the station, wearing uniforms I didn't recognise. But none took a second look at us or at any of the other frozen, waiting passengers. By now the Austrian station staff had gone home for the night—something I would have dearly loved to do also. I was very glad of my extra warm, Scottish Highlands woollen jersey, which I donned on top of my other clothing to keep out the chill.

What a relief to arrive at Keleti Train Station in Budapest. Of course there was no one to meet us, as nobody could tell any more how long the journey would take. So it was a taxi for us and finally back to my warm and comfortable room for a good sleep.

I had not expected the scene of confusion that greeted me the next day at the mission. Some staff wanted to return to their homes in Britain and elsewhere at once. Others had taken a few days off to digest the news of the war and to assess their and their families' circumstances. I could not blame them for this, as many had relatives in the affected countries.

But I'm pleased to say things have settled down now. Reverend Knight was very gracious in allowing those who needed to return to their homes to do so without delay, and we quickly found replacements. One thing about these times is that there is plenty of manpower, as so many people have become unemployed.

Thankfully Hungary remains uninvolved in the war and is an oasis for people fleeing from other countries. We already had refugees from Austria, Czechoslovakia, Germany, and some from Poland, but now that Poland has been taken over, I foresee further refugee problems. I know Poland has a large Jewish population, so what will happen to them? Surely Hungary won't have to look after all of them as well? Our resources are already stretched to capacity. But of course, we will try to help every soul who turns to this mission for help.

Given the increase in workload, especially in pastoring and counselling the Jewish families and refugees, the mission has taken on another pastor to assist Reverend Knight. Reverend Dr. Lajos (Louis) Nagybaczoni Nagy is a pastor with the Hungarian Reformed Church, and we are all very pleased to see our connection with that church strengthened in this way. The more help we can get from the local church the better, as the war may hinder contact with the committee in Scotland. Reverend Nagy has a real love for the Jewish people, and I understand he has been working for some time in the Jewish Quarter, attending to their needs. He often pops in to ask about one or other of my girls to see how they are getting along and to see if there is anything he can do for their families.

The rapid change of staff and the sense of unease generally have filtered through to the children, and there has been an increase in behaviour problems. The girls, especially the older ones, are bickering more, and I find I'm having to intervene more often in what seems to them to be a major crisis, but may only be that their best friend is no longer sitting with them at lunch. They are tending to form small, exclusive groups, which I have always discouraged. Several of the younger girls are having nightmares at night, and I have taken one child into my room for the present to try to settle her down. Everyone seems to be on edge. I am keeping the daily routine the same for the girls, which is helping a lot, and have spoken to several parents, inviting them to visit more often than the regular Sunday from eleven a.m. to five p.m. home visits the girls are usually allowed.

However, a steadily increasing number of girls are now effectively orphans with no fathers, either because their fathers have had to leave the country for work or have abandoned the marriage. Mothers may have died or likewise left the country to find work. For these little ones, who must feel so forsaken, I must try to be mother and father. Some days it can be quite exhausting.

Since my return from furlough, I have also noticed a change in the attitude of some people in Budapest to our mission. There seems to be growing opposition among Hungarian nationalists to what we are doing here, and I know it is because we have such a large number of Jewish children at the mission.

I can even sense it in the food markets where I buy the household groceries. My favourite butcher is less keen to spend a few minutes talking to me and so is the fruiterer. Am I imagining this? It may be that that opposition was always there, but now it is being expressed in public.

Recently there have been several editorials in newspapers that are very critical of presentations Reverend Knight and Gyula Forgács have made at public meetings. Often what they have said has been turned around or completely misquoted, and always, it is in relation to the Hungarian attitude to its Jewish population. When I read these editorials, I feel quite angry at the men who write them, and I know I have to get down on my knees and ask the Lord to forgive me for that. I am also becoming much more careful about who I talk to about the mission and what I say about it, not that I do any public speaking on the subject.

It seems wiser these days to omit to say most of our children are Jewish! How sad that is! But I remind myself that wisdom must prevail for the sake of these children.

April, 1940

My predictions were correct. We are being inundated with Jewish refugees from Poland and almost all the surrounding countries. Reverend Knight's face is now drawn, as he faces decisions he would never have wanted to make. He is in constant contact now on the refugee issue with the Hungarian Reformed Church and its leaders, as they can provide a local covering for us.

So far this year, we have had to turn several hundred children away from the home and school, as we are full to capacity.

We have 315 students, of whom forty-eight are boarders. In any other situation this would be a good report, but with so much need out there, we are all grieving that we cannot do more.

Pastoral counselling has become one of my major focuses this year. People are becoming desperate. The young Jewish men, including men with families, are being rounded up by the Hungarian government and assigned to what they call labour units and into the Hungarian army, which has been recently reorganised. Those deployed to work camps are being sent off to the north of Hungary. I know the Jews in the countryside are already extremely stressed by this initiative.

For some of our mission families also, this spells disaster. One mother came to me last week quite beside herself. I would describe her as desperate and on the point of giving up. She even threatened to do away with herself and her family of four children using poison.

"It's no use, Miss Haining. There's no help for us out there. We would be better off dead, all of us! Even the mission can't help us. We are done for! The government doesn't care what the happens to us, and we are at the mercy of marauding young people who break in and steal our last scrap of bread, destroy our homes, and assault us with impunity. No one is stopping them. Life is not worth it anymore!" she said. "I can't bear to see my children going through this."

This outburst was prompted by her husband's mobilisation into a labour unit. He was the only breadwinner, as she had been staying at home with two children under two years old. Once I had settled her down and checked that her family was safe—she had left them at home alone, such was her terror—I set about providing an immediate food parcel from the mission kitchen. This week we will simply have a little less to eat. The promise of practical help calmed her down considerably, and I have asked Gyula Forgács to keep an eye on her and her children.

Hungary, it seems, is moving towards an alliance with Germany. I'm wondering if our mission is going to be caught up in something much larger than any of us imagined. I remember the words of Mordecai to Esther in that lovely story of one woman's stand for her people against extreme odds. Mordecai says to Esther in Esther 4:14, "Who knows whether you didn't come into your royal position precisely for such a time as this."

I'm not exactly in a royal position as matron of the mission girls' home, but it seems the Lord has placed even the most humble of us in positions, which may well be vital for the survival of these dear Jewish friends we have here. We must live up to our calling!

June, 1940

I'm deeply saddened. Reverend Knight, on whom I had come to rely so much for wise counsel, has taken his family to safety in Britain, and unfortunately, because of the war situation, has found he cannot return alone as he had planned. Gyula Forgács is taking over.

I have taken solace in listening to the BBC and hearing the familiar English accent on my small wireless radio in the evenings, but I'm afraid, when it comes to the BBC news, I have not found much solace.

The Germans have invaded more countries, including Denmark and Norway, and I cannot imagine what they will do next. All of us in Budapest had hoped for an early end to this war, expecting that the Allied forces would quickly put a stop to this lunacy, but our hopes have been dashed with every new victory of the German forces.

However, the news that Neville Chamberlain has resigned and that Britain now has a new prime minister, Winston Churchill, is welcome. He speaks with great determination, just what is needed. Maybe now Britain will be able to stand strongly against the aggressor and we will see the tables turned in this conflict.

To be truthful, diary, and this is for you alone to know, I have had numerous messages from the Church of Scotland, asking me to return home. They say it isn't safe here for missionaries, but I have assured them I am as safe here as anywhere in the world. I am not confiding this to the staff or girls, who will only panic if they think I also could leave. The Jewish Committee contacted me on May 10 and again on May 24—persistent in their demand that I return home as they put it, "before it is too late." I ask myself, *Too late for what?* If I am here on God's assignment, then I am perfectly "on time!"

I replied very politely but firmly, saying I would take full responsibility for my decision to stay at my post in Budapest. The committee discussed this decision and came back with the following instruction:

"Leave at once. We have grave concerns for your safety and must insist on your immediate return to Scotland."

I'm standing my ground on this, knowing that there are still a number of British subjects and other foreigners here in Budapest beside myself, including my good, English speaking friend, Frances Warburton Lee, with whom I have spent much of my free time. . (I think she may be British – she has travelled to many countries and funnily enough I haven't checked her nationality.) Many of these foreigners have been attending the English language Sunday morning service at the mission. I have been in charge of these.

I am about to write to the Jewish Committee again to explain that the girls' home is actually doing better than other organisations in the city. Here, we have a degree of privilege in that we are not finding our work hampered by the government or by the rise in food and heating prices or by shortages of all sorts of commodities. With the needs increasing daily, it would be a sad thing for me to turn my back on the work at this stage.

Gyula Forgács has offered to write to the Jewish Committee also, explaining that local conditions actually favour my remaining here. Because of his strong connections with the Hungarian Reformed Church, which has not come under any censure from the rightist elements here, he can say this without fear of contradiction.

If this situation should change, I will deal with it then. I believe that, as a non-Jew, I am in no physical danger, and I cannot think why I would leave my girls at this time.

I opened my Bible yesterday to do my regular Bible reading, and the lovely bookmark made by Dorika* fell out. I reread it, and it reminded me that whatever our circumstances, we have no mandate to fear, only to believe.

I have repeated this message to Frances, who today insisted I should leave immediately, as my work with the Jewish children placed me in greater danger than most. I told her that I was the only English-speaking person left at the mission, so it was vitally important that I remain.

Gyula Forgács, Lajos Nagy, Miss Prém, and I have started having regular meetings to talk about the rising anti-Semitism. It can no longer be denied that this is a major problem in Hungary, as right-wing groups stage more demonstrations, and the government bows to their every demand.

Recently one of our Jewish contacts told me he had been visited by a militia that told him he was not allowed to sell sugar, flour, milk, butter, or any vegetables or meats in his grocery store. They ransacked the place and threw those items out into the yard behind his shop, making an incredible mess. They promised to be back the next week to check if he was infringing their rules.

"It's impossible to trade under these conditions," he said. "Shoppers will simply go elsewhere. I will be forced out of business."

Other Jewish businesses have had derogatory messages scrawled across their shop frontages, and one Jewish musician who tried busking in Vörösmarty tér (square) was badly beaten by a group of youths last month.

We have been told by Jews that they have been spat on in the street and many times pushed off the pavement onto the road, sometimes in front of oncoming traffic, by groups of young hoodlums. The Jews think these attacks are not random but that they are being watched, because the attacks happen after they emerge from the Jewish Quarter.

On the subject of being watched, though it does not bother me in the least, I have noticed that the authorities are remarkably aware of our comings and goings. There is often a police officer lingering in the street near the mission. But of course, that makes us safer in a way, as the hoodlums will not come near us while there is a police presence here.

October, 1940

We have had another delightful and blessed holiday at Lake Balaton. This time thirteen girls accompanied me and two other staff. I truly don't know how I would cope without those two months of rest, fun, and relaxation. I think it is the same for the girls.

Some of their parents joined us at the lake on weekends. I was delighted to see parents joining in with our Bible studies and services, totally of their own volition. While on holiday, we could reach not only the girls but their whole families, or at least the parts of the families still in Budapest.

On our return, we found one addition to the mission, prompted by the unstable political situation. An air raid shelter was completed at the back of the property while we were away. We now have to have regular practices to make sure every child knows how to find her way to it at the sound of the school bell. I trust that we will never have to use it except for practices.

December, 1940

The thing I most dreaded has happened. Hungary has succumbed to the carrot offered by Germany of regaining lands lost after World War I and has joined the Axis powers in this futile war.

Hungarian regent Admiral Horthy seems to have caved under the huge German pressure. There will be no stopping the rightist groups in this country now.

Gyula Forgács has reminded us all again to be very careful in what we say and do and to keep out of the way of officials and even of the police! He says we cannot trust anyone now that authority has been handed over to Fascist elements.

He told me of a meeting several years ago between the new right wing Nyilas (Arrow Cross) group and Reverend Knight at the mission. They apparently stormed in and commandeered Miss Prém's office, demanding to talk to the mission leaders. I think I was out at the time. The Nyilas had some papers, mostly reports on our staff meetings, which they said proved Reverend Knight has been working with foreign powers. Of course, Reverend Knight dismissed this accusation as ridiculous, and that was the end of that. I think the purpose of the visit was intimidation, but it did leave the senior management of the mission wondering how these documents had been obtained.

Hearing that put things in a different perspective. I have rearranged my day by making sure I go to the markets at different hours if possible, and I no longer send any of the girls on errands to the shops, which are just two blocks away. Our daily walks have been terminated, at least until we see just how safe the streets are for the girls, and we are offering short-term board for any mother who has been evicted from her home by authorities under one pretext or another, at least until she can be re-housed somewhere safe. The termination of the walks gives me more time in my day (so no more excuses for omitting to write in my diary) but I am keeping up all the other activities, including Sunday school and our special events.

The number of pupils has dropped again, mostly because the income-earning men from almost every family have been dispatched to the army or work camps, and families can no longer pay their fees. Contact with Scotland has become much harder, even as the need for more funds becomes critical, but I am very pleased that there is some contact through the Red Cross and Swiss authorities, who remain neutral. We, or I should say the mission leaders, are talking to them about those families who can't afford their fees and hope they will be able to channel funds from Scotland through to us. Meanwhile, I simply cut costs by shopping even more wisely and making do with what we already have.

A scripture pops into my mind as I write this—as often is the case. 2 Kings 4:2 says, "Elisha asked her, 'What should I do for you? Tell me, what do you have in the house?'"

I am no theologian, but as I meditate on that scripture, I'm reminded that often we have at our disposal all that we need in any situation. I'm applying that principal in all areas of management of the home and looking around for what I can use to plug the gaps that shortages have created.

With that in mind, I must prepare for our Christmas Eve celebrations. It will take more than a war and food shortages to make me give up celebrating the birth of our Saviour with the girls and seeing their shining faces as they open their presents.

This year the senior girls are putting on a little play about a modern-day Jesus born in the Jewish Quarter. I'm encouraging them in this as a healthy way of expressing what life is like for their families there and how Jesus brings the hope of change. Christmas carols will be interspersed throughout the performance, sung by our own mission choir. I am expecting it to be a very enjoyable evening and hope large numbers of parents will be able to attend.

April, 1941

Hungary is undergoing a major crisis. Our Prime Minister Pál Teleki committed suicide at the start of this month, prompted by German demands to be allowed to cross our land to attack Yugoslavia. This is the same man who acquiesced to the Jewish laws being passed here.

I think the final straw for him was that he thought he'd made a treaty with the Germans that would allow Hungary to determine for itself when and where it would go to war for the Axis cause. But Germany has proved to be nothing less than a very powerful bully, ignoring all agreements.

We now have an even more pro-Nazi government, with the result that not only did Germany attack Yugoslavia across Hungarian territory, but Hungarian troops found themselves part of that invasion.

It is one thing to be at war with a country a long distance away (rumour has it that a joint attack by Germany and Hungary against Russia is about to be launched) but we are now facing a war involving some of our historical arch enemies, right on our doorstep. We are becoming surrounded.

September, 1941

Well, I have put paid to any ideas of returning to Britain, if I had harboured any such ideas in the back of my mind.

Today, given that at least ten of the girls have need of new shoes (and I wish young girls' feet would not grow quite so quickly), I have laid waste to my large suitcase, which is of soft leather. It will provide excellent material for the soles of new shoes for our poorer girls. Funnily enough, I'm pleased to see the suitcase go. Perhaps it reminded me of a possibility of escape from this city, which I love so much, that is becoming more and more isolated from the other world I know.

I have also asked some helpers to unwind the wool from jerseys that no longer fit the smallest children and combine it to knit larger ones. At least we will get several good-sized jerseys from that, even if their colour schemes are a little unusual.

In my spare time I now take walks along the River Duna bank, watching the silent mass of water flow under the many bridges that cross it, and remind myself of God's inexorable plan for Budapest and those who live in it. I feel the Lord especially close to me at such times, and I am revitalised and find hope stirring within me again in the face of all the troubles afflicting us. How important the scriptures are to me at this time and especially those which speak of God's good plans for us:

> "For I know the plans I have in mind for you," says ADONAI, "plans for well-being, not for bad things; so that you can have hope and a future. When you call to me and pray to me, I will listen to you. When you seek me, you will find me, provided you seek me wholeheartedly; and I will let you find me," says ADONAI. "Then I will reverse your exile. I will gather you from all the nations and places where I have driven you," says ADONAI, "and bring you back to the place from which I exiled you."

> Jeremiah 29:11-14

I have come to understand in a new way since working with the Jewish people in Budapest that this scripture is not just for me, or even just for the Church, but more importantly, it is God's promise to his chosen people, among whom I am so privileged to work. Right now, Jews are streaming into Hungary, but from this scripture, I can see God wants to take them not just to Hungary but back to the Promised Land. Oh that I could help them on that journey!

Later

I am again prompted to come to my diary by a political event, despite the fact that I have as little interest in politics as anyone I know here.

The third Jewish law has just been passed, and just like a déjà vu experience, it is a replica of the law passed in Germany before the war, prohibiting Jews marrying Aryans or having sexual relations with them. My previous comments stand on this issue. I am incensed by the injustice.

The girls' home continues to take in more boarders. We have increased numbers dramatically this year, as Jews seek somewhere safe for their children to be educated. So of course I am very busy welcoming new ones and settling them in, helping them to adjust to getting up at a set time in the morning, eating regular meals (some were only getting one meal a day at home), and attending to such important details as making their beds and tidying their dorms. While the home lives of many of the girls are chaotic, at the mission we are firm in applying order to all our activities. It brings a sense of security to the girls.

I met a very interesting person in July when visiting the Hungarian municipality offices to check that my papers were in order—all foreigners are required to do this regularly. While waiting in the long queue, I struck up a conversation with a Swedish gentleman, who comes to Budapest regularly on business. In fact, he said he had ambitions to reside here. His name was Raoul Wallenberg, and he said he worked for a Swedish importing company owned by a Hungarian Jew.

Despite being told to be most careful not to share details of our work with others here, I felt I could tell him just a little about the mission. After all, he is from a neutral country, and there may well be a means to obtain aid for the mission through him. He was fascinated by what we are doing and said he'd like to keep in touch with our mission leaders. I do believe, and I think this is a prompting from the Lord, that he will follow up on that. I have passed this information on to Dr. Lajos Nagy—Gyula Forgács is very unwell at present.

November, 1941

It is with sadness that I have to report that dear Gyula Forgács died last week, and we have spent many days comforting those in the mission to whom he meant so much as well as, of course, his family and Hungarian Reformed Church members. The girls were greatly upset also, with many coming to me for a little cry and a reassuring cuddle, especially the youngest ones who don't have any real concept of death and the hereafter yet.

We have had to form a new mission's council to fill the large gap left by this dear man. I have somehow found myself on it, along with Margit Prém and Dr. Alexander Nagy of the Hungarian Reformed Church. Our role is to make sure liaison with the Reformed Church is seamless. Bishop Ravasz has made a point of telling me, probably because I am the only foreigner now in a leadership role here, that I am definitely under the protection of the Reformed Church. There is a legal agreement to this effect. That makes me more comfortable in taking this role.

I have heard disturbing reports from refugees who have fled from German-occupied lands. They say that Jews now have to wear a distinguishing yellow star on their outer clothing, which of course makes them easy targets for the hoodlums and even for the Nazi-controlled police. They have also brought tales of a huge massacre of Jews, about twenty thousand shot, which is beyond belief. These Jews, who lived in Galicia, once part of the Hungarian-Austrian Empire, had been stripped of their Hungarian citizenship, apparently because our very right-wing government could not trust them to support it. They were rounded up and handed over to the Germans. The worst part, they say, is that not only German troops but also Hungarians took part in the massacre.

I find it hard to understand why these things happen. I hope and pray they will not happen on Hungarian soil.

The Noose Tightens

Diary of Jane Haining

January, 1942

Another Christmas gone, and I start a new year wondering what it will bring. My very good friend Margit Prém retired as headmistress of the Higher School at the end of last year, and of course it fell to me to provide a special lunch for her farewell.

Not that she is going anywhere—it is very difficult now to move around Hungary, much less around Europe. So I, selfishly, am delighted that she will remain here, and we will still be able to share many an afternoon tea together as we discuss the direction of the mission in these fast changing times.

It is very hard to keep up with what is happening. I am suffering from an overload of information about events in the world and in people's lives, much of which is not corroborated.

The latest news relates to the war on the Russian front. Hungary has become disastrously involved with this, just as the rumours suggested. Stories brought back from the front have brought me to tears many a night recently as I knelt before the Lord to pray. These have come from a few Hungarian soldiers who have been released from duty at the Russian front because of injury. Those who have no animosity to the Jews have been horrified by what they have seen.

They tell not only of huge losses of soldiers but also of battalions of Jewish men, young and old, sent into battle as decoys. The Hungarian army is a new army and is not properly equipped, so these poor souls have been sent into battle without weapons, they say. Worse still, if that is possible, the army is using them as mine detectors, forcing them to cross mine fields ahead of the main army. Of course, they are blown up by the mines, and it is then safe for the other Hungarian battalions to make the transition. It is even rumoured that orders have been given at the highest level of government that no Jews should escape with their lives at the Russian front! So a Jew managing to cross a mine field uninjured will be shot in the back by the following Hungarian troops.

At first, I could not believe these stories and thought the soldiers must have been primed by the army to bring these stories back to frighten the Jewish population. That thought still lingers in my mind, as we can no longer trust anyone, including those in authority, to be telling the truth. The corruption and lack of integrity in the governments of these days is beyond belief.

But the more I consider this, I can see no benefit in frightening the Hungarian Jews. Already many of the remaining men who have heard these rumours are going into hiding. I'm told they are getting documents from somewhere saying they are Christians. The Jewish community does what it can to help them, but it is relatively powerless, as raids are happening almost daily to round up any remaining men for labour camps and army service.

Several of my Christian friends have confided in me that they have been sheltering some of these men, but they are very afraid that the Nyilas will find out and raid their homes.

At the mission, praise God, we continue to be untouched by the threat of lawlessness from roving gangs in this city. I'm sure the Lord is protecting us, helped in no small measure by the oversight of the Reformed Church.

June, 1942

The Church of Scotland has appointed Dr. Lajos Nagy as head of the mission, in the belief that a local pastor will shield the mission better than our little council.

One of his first moves has been to suspend the conversion classes required by those seeking to become baptised as Christians. Many are lining up to do so. He says although we would never normally advocate baptisms without proof of a real faith and solid teaching to lead the candidate to that faith, we cannot apply such rules in these dire times. I'm inclined to agree.

Now he is handing out baptismal certificates to any Jews who want them, in the hope that the authorities will not find out these people are Jews. Of course that puts the mission at risk, should the authorities discover what we are doing, but the situation has deteriorated so badly here that such risks are necessary. We cannot stand by and watch the persecution of our dear Jewish friends without doing something, no matter how little, to help. And of course we are praying over each certificate that it might indeed protect its owner from these raids.

I have made contact with several of these Jews in hiding, finding them a great source of provisions for the home. I will not disclose here how or where I make contact, even though I keep this diary in the most secure place, as the discovery of that information by the authorities would be disastrous. Some young Jews have combined into smuggling bands and are bringing food supplies across the Romanian border at great risk to their own lives. But for them, it is either that or die on the streets of starvation. They cannot use their own papers, which identify them as Jews, to buy food in the shops. The risk of going to such places would be too great anyway, as there are informers everywhere. The government is encouraging Hungarians to inform on any Jews they find, especially if they are without satisfactory papers. So most of the Jews in hiding move around only at night.

August, 1942

In a perverse sort of way, I am delighted with a recent development in my life. Not only am I matron of a girls' home in a war-stricken foreign country, but I am now a humanitarian aid worker to the Allied prisoners held in camps in the south of that country. Never in my life did I imagine I would be doing such a thing!

Best of all, and this is important to me, this activity is totally legal and approved by the authorities, under the auspices of the Swedish Red Cross.

I accompany Reverend Lajos Nagy on his regular weekly visits to these camps, armed with money, books, simple medicines, and even wireless radios. These are all supplied to us through the Red Cross. I have no idea where they are getting them from, but I suspect some of these items are being funnelled through various neutral legations—Swiss, Swedish, and maybe even Spanish.

The prisoners are overjoyed to see us each week and very keen to hear what is happening with the war effort. Unfortunately, I can only repeat what I hear on the BBC news, and I'm aware that must be heavily censored for security reasons. However, I think the more important news that I share with them is the message of hope in our Redeemer. There is no censoring that.

Last week a prisoner reached into his pocket and brought out a photo of his wife and children to show me. "Look at that, missus," he said with a proud grin. "Them's me family back home."

He pointed to the group, a young woman with a stylish hairdo and two smiling toddlers sitting on a sandy beach. His face became wistful, and a tear trickled down from his eye. "I miss 'em so much," he muttered.

It breaks my heart to see how the prisoners look at those photos and it reminds me also of my family so far away. Contact with my sisters and friends in Scotland is now minimal, although I'm sure any important news would be passed through our usual diplomatic channels.

We had a visit recently from a Mr. Carl Lutz, just appointed vice-consul of the Swiss legation here in Budapest. He was led to us through his Red Cross contacts. He told us about his time in Yafo (Jaffa) in Palestine, where he learnt much about the Zionist cause and the desire of the Jews there to bring all of the persecuted European Jews home to Israel. My heart leapt with hope as he talked, but he quickly explained that there would need to be a lot of help from other countries to extract the Jews from the web the Nazis have woven around them. Those who had not already made the journey, he said, would need to think about finding ways to last out the war in hiding wherever they were.

Discussion then turned to how the mission could help in this and various suggestions were made about making the mission a refuge for Jews. This would be, of course, a very dangerous path to take, as the Nyilas, with the full support of the government, are executing anyone they consider to be collaborators—that generally means anyone supporting the Jews.

We decided to watch the situation carefully, not wanting to expose our girls or the work of the mission in the Jewish Quarter to such extreme risk. Our role could well be as contacts for other agencies doing that sort of work, as we obviously have established strong and trusted contact with the local Jewish community through the school.

Again I am forced back to the reality of life here in Budapest and the need to take one day at a time, to think and plan more carefully for the home, and to get on with the job at hand.

I am finding it very hard to find ways to comfort girls whose fathers have been suddenly hauled off to join the labour units. Often these children have been present when the authorities have come to take them. They tend to come at night-time, when they know the family will be home, so the children see the fear and desperation on the faces of the adults. No one actually knows what is happening at these work camps, so most women are living in hope that their men folk will be well fed and looked after there, perhaps having more to eat than they do at home. I cannot, and should not, say anything that will take away that faint hope, despite some indications that conditions in these camps are very harsh. It is only hope that keeps those left behind alive.

Meanwhile, the mission remains an oasis of calm and hope in the storm.

December, 1942

Politics again! There is a new prime minister and more trouble for our Jewish population! I am tired of having these incidents interrupt and confine the work of the mission here in Budapest and the lives of those working in it.

I suppose I had better explain the latest trouble. I have just found out, through the mission contacts with the Red Cross, that Germany has called for a final solution to what they call the Jewish problem. Although I'm not sure what they mean by a final solution, it sounds very ominous to me. Rumours are rife that our own Hungarian government, under Prime Minister Miklós Kállay, has bowed again to Nazi demands and has agreed to resettle about 800 thousand Hungarian speaking Jews from central Europe. No one knows what resettlement means—is it good or bad? Nor does anyone know where they would have to move to.

But I'm certain the Germans do not envisage the final solution that I dream of and that the Bible speaks of, which involves the Jews finally, freely returning to their homeland, the ancient Israel, from the nations of the world and welcoming their Messiah as he returns to reign on this earth.

Some of the mission's Jewish families would like to return to Palestine, but most say they cannot leave at this time, even if it were possible, because they want to remain as close as possible to the work camps their men folk have been transported to. They live in the hope of the men being released soon or of joining them in those places, despite there being little factual information about what these camps are and how the men are faring there.

I have found the perfect scripture for these times. In Romans 5:3 it says,

> Let us also boast in our troubles; because we know that trouble produces endurance, endurance produces character, and

character produces hope; and this hope does not let us down, because God's love for us has already been poured out in our hearts through the Ruach Hakodesh,[3] who has been given to us.

If there was ever a time we—and by *we*, I mean the mission and all those we are supporting here—needed hope, it is now.

As you may have noticed, diary, I am becoming more and more dependent on the Scriptures to sustain me and keep me smiling and strong in the face of all sorts of daily difficulties. The Lord is so faithful, producing a verse or a psalm whenever I begin to feel overwhelmed. These remind me that our God is far greater than any of the difficulties that surround us. Many mornings now, I wake up with a psalm ringing in my head, almost like a morning alarm or wake-up call. The words and the tune stay with me throughout the day, so much so that others are now commenting that I am humming the same tune over and over. I was unaware I was humming so loudly.

To my delight, I often find one or other of the girls, often the smallest ones, singing along with me as they go about their morning chores. It is clear evidence that regular teaching of the psalms and Scriptures does not fall on deaf ears as these children know almost as many psalms as I do now!

June, 1943

Today was our weekly weighing day for the hostel girls, and I was horrified to note, despite my best efforts, that many have lost weight instead of gaining it.

I am convinced that we have an adequate diet, despite the difficulties and food shortages—now only Nyilas and government officials can shop for whatever they want. The rest of us have to form long queues for basics such as bread, cabbage, beans, maize flour, and sugar. I will have to renew my efforts to find fresh vegetables and a little fruit. I am trying to find a source of these in the countryside, but at the moment, we lack a vehicle that could go to pick them up.

I am wondering if the weight loss is due more to the stress over changing family circumstances than to diet. Most families no longer have a father present. Most mothers are trying to earn a few pengo wherever they can.

I talked to Ibolya* yesterday at the Former Pupils' Club. She lived in our girls' home until she was fourteen, when she had to leave. She told me her father was sent to a work camp last month, and, since then, her mother has been working distributing newspapers. That means the children have to get up very early in the morning to help their mother with this work. Ibolya was very unhappy about the family circumstances, missing her father very much, and very worried about her mother's health. She told me the one light in her life was the regular Former Pupils' Club meetings, which she still attends regularly.

I am very thankful that most of the girls are still able to attend this club, despite the increased responsibility put on their young shoulders by having to help their mothers or aunts or whoever is looking after them with child-minding and household chores. Few can find jobs to bring in money to boost the family budget.

Another former student came to visit me last Christmas. Elizabeth* turned up quite unexpectedly; she had left Budapest and is now training in Kecskemét to be a teacher. The home was empty when she arrived, as most of the girls had gone home for a few days' break, and I had arranged for other families to take the girls who had no homes.

I was sitting in my office with the door open, using this uninterrupted and peaceful time to pack some parcels for our British prisoners of war in the south, and, I'm afraid, I was shedding a tear or two as I thought of how lonely these men must be so far from home.

The next thing I knew, Elizabeth's warm, ruddy face was peeking around the doorway. She obviously noticed my reddened eyes, but as her gaze dropped onto the parcels spread over the floor, her face softened, she wrapped her young arms around me, and sat down on the floor to help. Together we packed about thirty parcels with whatever items we could find that might be of use to them—a little tinned food, some warm winter socks, pen and paper, and some reading materials in English.

We talked a lot about how things were for her now that she was out in the big, wide world and remembered the good and the bad times in the girls' home.

"Do you remember, Miss Haining, the time I had scarlet fever so badly that you took me into your room overnight before sending me to hospital?" she asked. "I was scared I was going to die!"

"Yes, you were quite a worry to us that night," I said, and with a smile added, "And do you remember the time when I made you sit at the cat table for a whole week for your meals? You weren't very happy about that at the time either!" We both laughed.

The cat table is for those who can't get out of bed in time for breakfast. Elizabeth still holds the record as the most persistent cat.

As we stood to embrace before she left, she told me a precious thing that brought more tears to my eyes—this time tears of joy. She said that the girls' home had formed her, had taught her about love, beauty, knowledge, and prevailing faith, and that she would never forget what we had done for her here.

I am delighted that Ibolya and Elizabeth and quite a number of the other past pupils have held onto their faith and their sense of being wanted after leaving the home, despite stepping out into a world full of challenges and anti-Semitism. Surely our work here is not in vain.

December, 1943

Another short entry, as I am rushed off my feet trying to source food and clothing for the girls' home, and I'm also searching high and low for such basic school needs as pencils and paper so they can continue their studies.

Everything you can think of is in short supply. Toilet paper has long since disappeared from shop shelves, and we now use tissue paper taken from boxes of fruit and vegetables—when we can get those.

Every cloth, every scrap of material is now converted into something useful from dusters and cleaning cloths to bandages and strappings. Nothing can be wasted.

I have taken to getting up early in the morning once a week, sometimes about four in the morning, to make the journey to a fruit and vegetable market a little out of the centre of the city. If you are not one of the first in the queue nowadays, you simply miss out, as even the wholesalers and farmers are short of produce to sell. Fortunately, the buses run at this hour. I have developed some of the strongest arm muscles of anyone in the mission, I think, from hauling bags of produce onto and off the bus and carrying them home each week.

I need to be home well before breakfast time to ensure all the girls are out of bed and suitably attired for their day at school. I also always do a dormitory inspection before they are allowed downstairs to start their day of study. Life and routine must go on, whatever the extra burdens life throws at us.

My next major job is to write the girls' home end-of-year reports for each girl. These are placed inside the school report and describe the girls' progress in such matters as politeness, serving spirit, satisfaction or happiness, table manners, and tidiness and include an overall summary of achievement, socially and behaviourally. The parents find these reports particularly helpful in assessing the all-round development of their daughters.

I also have decisions to make about the staff we will have next year. One or two of the staff at the school have shown signs of discriminating between the Jews and Christians (discriminatory behaviour is so easily caught when the society you live in behaves like that every day). We don't want that to happen in the girls' home. It may just be an unkind word here or there, a silly joke, or omitting to include a Jewess in an activity, but much damage can be done by these things. These young ladies are now supersensitive to any sign of discrimination.

Some of the girls are losing any confidence they had as they watch their families being treated as second-class citizens. I'm particularly worried about Greta* and Susannah,* both of whom no longer make eye contact with adults. I am insisting they do so with me. When they do, they discover a very warm response is waiting for them. It will take some months before we can wean them off this behaviour, and I need loving staff who will make an extra effort to draw these young girls out.

The most important thing every girl in this home must learn is that they are all equal, irrespective of race or origin, and they can absolutely trust that they will be treated as such as long as they are living here. I will defend their right to this to my dying day.

Jane Haining, left, with her sisters, Alison, centre, and Margaret.

Jane Haining as a young woman.

The Dunscore farm house, where Jane was born and grew up, as it is today.

Dumfries Academy, as it is today. The picture shows the original part which would have been much the same in Jane's day.

Queens Park West Church, as it is today. The interior has been changed considerably through renovation.

Vorosmarty School and courtyard as they are today.

Jane with some of her Girls' Home charges at Vorosmarty School; exact date unknown.

*A modern day reconstruction of the Birkenau Concentration Camp men's dormitory –
a reminder of the conditions under which inmates lived.*

The medal which was posthumously awarded to Jane Haining when she was named as one of the Righteous Among the Nations, by Yad Vashem Holocaust Museum in Jerusalem.

The plinth erected in Jane's memory in Dunscore Village.

Jane's Bible and a book titled Wayside and Woodland Blossoms, found in a safe at St Columba's Church, Budapest, in 2010.

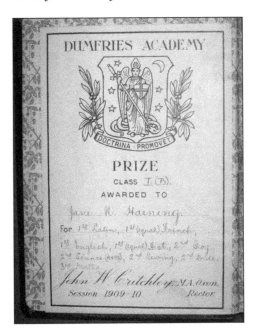

Inscription on Jane's Bible, found in a safe at St Colomba's Church, Budapest, in 2010.

Book prize, titled Wayside and Woodland Blossoms, *awarded at Dumfries Academy and found in a safe at St Colomba's Church, Budapest, in 2010.*

Jane's hand written will, dated August 2, 1942, discovered in the attic of the Church of Scotland headquarters, Edinburgh in September, 2016.

Jane with some of her charges, date unknown.

Jane with some of her charges, date unknown.

Desperate Days

Diary of Jane Haining

February, 1944

I return to my diary much afflicted of spirit. Outside my bedroom window I can watch, any day, groups of ultra-right wing youths wandering down Vörösmarty utca as though they own it, pushing aside anyone who stands in their way and generally making a nuisance of themselves. These are mostly unemployed youths who, for some reason, are not called up to serve in the army, so one must suspect they have the implicit support of the government to carry on as they do. The police simply look the other way.

Despite the cold winter weather, there have been a number of rallies by these young people, with much flag waving, shouting, and chanting of slogans, some of which have been anti-Semitic. They draw large crowds, including families with children who seem to want to hear their rhetoric about how the Hungarian people must stand up for their independence and sovereignty and reclaim the surrounding territory, once owned by Hungary, for the sake of the generations to come. Anything that stands in the way of this—for that you can read Jews and Roma people (Gypsies)—must be done away with.

Despite all this, the government seems to be softening its approach to the Allies, or at least, that is what I hear from the diplomatic missions still here in Budapest. There is even a rumour that Prime Minister Kállay wants to change sides in the war, because the Allies have finally turned the tide and won some important victories. The BBC has been full of these reports. The most important for Hungary has been the relief of Leningrad after a mammoth siege—about 900 days I'm told. Also, the Allies are now in Italy and moving north. What wonderful news! Surely the war will be over very soon. Shortly we will not have to worry about these gangs roaming the streets.

But I do want it to be the British who liberate Europe. From what I have heard, the Russians, who are advancing fast from the north, have also committed some atrocities in this war, and I quail at the thought of such a powerful army walking the beautiful streets of Budapest (or Prague, where I spent a wonderful Christmas seven years ago). Would they respect and protect the magnificent architecture of either of these cities, or, more importantly, the inherent gentleness of Budapest's large Jewish population?

Perhaps I am getting ahead of myself, thinking of the day of Europe's liberation but you, diary, will understand how much it means to us all here. Despite this good news on many battle fronts, some people here are making contingency plans—seemingly planning for the worst. Do they know something I don't know?

Because of my experience as private secretary at J&P Coats in Glasgow, Dr. Lajos Nagy has asked me to take shorthand notes at some of his meetings with various parties involved in schemes to help the Jews of Budapest. While he is not one of the main instigators of any of the plans, he sees himself as an essential contact for the schemes because, as a Hungarian, he understands the Hungarian authorities and can speak to them in their own language.

Meetings are dangerous as, at any time, the police or Nyilas could burst in just as they did some years ago to confront Reverend

Knight at the mission. The venue for meetings changes each time, and we never arrive at exactly the same time, in order to be as inconspicuous as possible. It has also fallen to me to pass on communications from Dr. Nagy to various people, as I am the least conspicuous of them all and regularly move around the city sourcing provisions for the girls' home.

Through these meetings, I have become aware of more and more activity on the part of Carl Lutz from the Swiss Legation in relation to documents he calls protective Swiss passports for the Jews. The businessman I met some time ago, Raoul Wallenberg, is also frequently here. Both men are in close contact with Dr. Lajos Nagy.

I believe they are planning ways to get the Jews out of Hungary, possibly in conjunction with the local Zionist movement. Others, including a Catholic nun[4] and an Italian who has somehow become a Spanish citizen and is now the diplomatic representative of Spain in Budapest[5] are independently making plans to hide the Jews. It is all very piecemeal and could be very dangerous for the Jews they are trying to help. There are so many plans for false documents to be produced, I'm not sure what the government will think when they are finally distributed; it could be too obvious a ploy.

At first, I felt quite unsure, even a little frightened, by these activities and my role in the meetings, but I must confess that I am beginning to enjoy this opportunity to do something practical to help the Jews in their dire situation. I have told no one of this new aspect of my life. There is a war saying, "Loose lips sink ships," and this truly applies to us here in Budapest.

However, as far as I can determine, the worst the authorities are doing to those foreign nationals whom they deem to be security risks is deporting them to one of the neutral countries after a short interrogation and perhaps a few days in prison.

116

So I am confident that the good of these enterprises far outweighs the risk. In any case, I have a Protector who will never leave me and is more powerful than anything the enemy, whether the Hungarian police or the Nyilas, can bring against me. There, I rest my case!

March, 1944

Disaster! The Germans are here. It is Hungary's worst nightmare. They jackbooted their way into the city at four in the morning on March 19, just a week ago, and life as we know it here has come to a standstill.

The girls were terrified. All but the youngest of them woke up because of the horrendous noise of tanks and armoured vehicles passing along the main thoroughfare, Andrássy út, less than fifty metres from our mission. I called them all together in the senior dormitory—they were already awake and out of their beds—and tried to comfort them. Although I don't know what comfort anyone can find in such an event.

The most important thing was to keep the girls from panicking. So I told them about the German presence in our city; an urgent message had come through just an hour before from Dr. Nagy explaining the situation and suggesting nobody leave the home in the morning in case of demonstrations and unrest on the streets. I told the girls that, for them, nothing would change, that they would continue their schooling here at the mission, that we were under the protection of the Reformed Church, and that nobody would do us any harm. May it be that I spoke the truth!

Then I suggested we sing some of our favourite psalms. That was the medicine we all needed. We produced a good strong chorus between us and felt our spirits rise again. The girls, now calm, soon went back to bed to await the dawn. It is truly amazing how resilient children are.

For the next few days, I was somewhat nervous going out to shop for provisions, wondering if I would be stopped by the new German patrols in the streets and whether some of my food contacts would still be available in these new circumstances. Several were nowhere to be found, but I managed to get enough bread, milk, and stringy cabbage to make some sort of meal for us. Quite a number of businesses had their shutters down, although I could hear people inside. Caution was clearly on everyone's mind.

I'm relieved to report that within the mission itself, life has gone on as usual for the past week—except for one incident. Yesterday, I got up early, as is my habit, only to discover a man on the premises. It has long been the rule at the mission that only single women could stay overnight because of the presence of the girls' home in the building. Consequently, no married staff could live on the premises. So imagine my surprise when I found Schréder, whom I instantly recognised as the son-in-law of our cook and housekeeper, Mrs. Kovacs, sitting in the kitchen eating breakfast. I had met him several times previously, when he'd popped in to the mission.

I was infuriated. He was tucking into a huge breakfast of bread and eggs and had obviously stayed overnight in the mission with his mother-in-law. That was bad enough, but, given that I had been searching high and low in the city since four in the morning for food to stock the larder for the next few days, I was not impressed with the sight of our precious food disappearing into this man's mouth! I have no idea where the eggs came from.

I let him know exactly what I thought of his behaviour in not asking permission (which would have been refused) to stay overnight.

"So what exactly do you think you are doing here in our kitchen at six in the morning, tucking into our precious mission food? And who gave you permission to be here? I can see you have stayed overnight, and you must know that is strictly against the rules."

"What's it to you, if I stay here from time to time?" A sneer crept across his face. "The Germans are now in control here, not you, and I'm now a member of the Nyilas. You would do well to speak politely to me in future. Nyilas members have the right to demand food and lodgings wherever they choose. We've just been drafted back from the countryside to Budapest, and I expect you to provide full board for me for as long as I'm here."

I was astounded by his arrogant response. Though I am not much more than five feet and three inches tall, I very nearly took the dustpan and did something violent with it!

Mrs. Kovacs, who was obviously hugely embarrassed by his behaviour, sidled out of the kitchen and left us to our discussion. I removed his unfinished plate of food from in front of him and ordered him off the premises. I think he, in turn, was so startled by my boldness, despite my diminutive size, that he got up and left. I summoned Mrs. Kovacs and told her he was never again to be lodged at the mission, no matter what his reason. She apologised profusely. Clearly she was terrified of him and the newfound power he wielded as a Nyilas member. I am praying we do not have another visit from this young man.

Tomorrow, I'm meeting with my friend Frances Warburton Lee. She has indicated some concerns about her security, saying she has been asked to report to the authorities to show her papers. Normally there would be no problem, as her papers are in order, and that is all that is required of foreign nationals, but nobody knows what this new regime will do. I will support her and encourage her, especially to have faith in God and trust in Him for her safety.

119

We have just found out that the Germans detained the train of the Hungarian regent, Miklós Horthy, on the Austrian side of the border as he returned home, the night they invaded Hungary. He had gone to Germany to talk to Hitler and to turn down proposals the Führer put to him to bring Hungary further under German control. No wonder the Germans entered the country so easily, with our head of state safely out of the way and other government officials unsure of what was happening. Regent Horthy is back here now and trying to set up a new government, which is not easy; many ministers are refusing to serve in the government of an occupied country, as is the status of Hungary now. I sympathise with these ministers. It is not in my nature to compromise on important issues, and I'm sure they will have to do a lot of that if they agree to become part of the new government!

Considering the changed circumstances in Budapest, I am going to find my diary a new home. I have decided to ask Miss Prém, a Hungarian, to be its guardian, so that it doesn't reside in the girls' home any more. That is the safest place I can think of for it.

As I have written over the years, I have become attached to this memoir. I do not share my thoughts or feelings easily with others, as I have never craved the attention of others, but that does not mean I do not have those thoughts and feelings. Writing them down helps me to process them, after which I can move on to the next thing that needs my attention. As ever, I am practical in all I do.

Two Days Later

I was called in to Reverend Nagy's office yesterday and given some horrific news.

"The government has just issued an edict saying all Jews in Hungary must wear the Star of David, or suffer serious consequences," he said. "I know this is a terrible thing, but we have no choice in this matter."

I was given the order to immediately start sewing yellow Stars of David on the outer garments of the Jewish girls at the mission. I could not believe this was happening. I left the office with tears of rage mixed with sorrow brimming in my eyes.

I'm still in shock. The new government has acceded to all the German demands and has issued an order that these stars must be worn by all Jews in public places by the end of the week. Checks of identity papers will be done regularly in the streets, and any Jew over six years old found not wearing the star will be immediately arrested and processed for transportation—no one knows where or for what.

My spirit recoils at the thought of my own hands being used, against my every wish, to facilitate this gross act of discrimination. But in these circumstances I have no choice if the girls are to remain safe. I may not be politically astute, but it is not hard to see that this new requirement will only make discrimination easier against these dear ones, who have done nothing whatsoever to deserve such treatment.

Today, as I threaded my needle and picked up the first of the pile of winter coats in front of me, tears began rolling down my cheeks. I hadn't cried like this since my baby sister Helen's death, when I was just six years old. Only eighteen months after my mother's death, it was the death of this tiny innocent child that drove a knife into my heart and brought out the flood of tears I had needed to cry. Now, as I began this abhorrent task, I was grieving with that same intensity.

Despite my very private nature, I'm afraid my sobs attracted the attention of Mrs. Kovacs, who looked rather alarmed as she skittered past my door. I gained some control over myself but still could not contain the tears. I'm afraid some of the jackets have tear stains now, which will be hard to explain to the girls if they see them. I must on no account let them see my grief, as they are still so innocent. My role is to protect them, not frighten them. A verse comes to mind again, as I write this.

> If I raise my eyes to the hills, from where will my help come?
> My help comes from ADONAI, the maker of heaven and earth.
> He will not let your foot slip—your guardian is not asleep. No,
> the guardian of Isra'el never slumbers or sleeps.

Psalm 121:1-4

These verses have been a recurring theme in my life, I think because they bring back memories of the happiest moments of my early childhood, when I got the occasional chance to roam the craggy hills above Dunscore. I felt the strong presence of the Lord there as I climbed, sure footed as a goat. Back then, it almost seemed to me that God lived in those hills. Of course it didn't take me long to realise that was not exactly so, but rather that His Spirit lived inside me!

I often stop now at the mission entranceway and say this psalm to myself, as I venture into the street, partly to remind myself of God's constant oversight over all I do and partly as a prayer over the Jewish people in the city.

But something has impacted me this evening. As I reread the words "the guardian of Isra'el," I realise that the Lord has appointed me specifically to guard that small part of Israel that comprises the girls in our home. This is a formidable responsibility, which increases daily as events unfold here in Budapest. There is no room for weakness or vacillation. I must rely ever increasingly on that eternal guardian who "never slumbers or sleeps" if I am to fulfil my role.

One Day Later

We have had the most disturbing news from the Jewish Quarter. Parents have told me that some Jews are planning to avoid wearing the Star of David, risking swift punishment by the Germans and their Nyilas allies (some of these Jews have already disappeared), while others have given up hope and have committed suicide.

This is extremely serious news, and I am now considering suggesting that all the girls remain in the home at weekends as well as during the week to protect them from all this trauma. Increasing numbers of girls have no home to go to anyway, as fathers are hauled off to work camps or just disappear and mothers struggle to find work to survive.

They also tell me that the Germans are commandeering Jewish owned property—shops and homes—putting the owners out into the street. Further, the Germans now say Hungarian Aryans may not be employed in an establishment where Jews are living, which raises major questions about our staff at the home.

Our one Hungarian Aryan is Mrs. Kovacs. She has been a faithful employee here, although I have had occasion to reproach her for gossiping to parents. I will need to inform her that she is no longer allowed to work here, but before I do that, I will endeavour to find her alternative employment. She is a widow who needs a job to support herself. I have a number of contacts who may be helpful.

The Next Day

I am very glad to say I have already found suitable employment for Mrs. Kovacs. I'm very pleased as it goes against my principles to ask someone who has worked well to leave, just because the government has brought in yet another anti-Jewish ruling. Aryan Hungarians are also suffering because of these laws, as the Germans move Jews around the city and countryside. Everywhere they go, they are displacing some Aryans. Where will this stupidity end?

Mrs. Kovacs took the news of the termination of her employment here well, and I think she will settle quickly into the new position, which is as a housekeeper for a local family.

Today, I handed over my diary to Margit Prém, who has promised to keep it for me until such time as we have peace again in Europe. That is the one precaution I am taking at this time, as I realise there are things I have written that may not be approved by our Nazi overlords, yet I want them to remain on record. I will continue my writings on loose-leaf paper, which can easily be concealed or disposed of if need be.

There is little else I can do under the circumstances to protect either myself or the girls. Reverend Nagy has given me a Swiss safe conduct pass, which I have reluctantly accepted.

"Miss Haining, please take this pass. We can no longer guarantee your safety, or anyone else's, in this city," he said. "The situation has changed for the worse. We are at the mercy of the Germans now, and it is impossible to predict what they will do next."

"But I have a low profile here. They don't even know who I am," I argued.

"Even so," he said, "you could be in danger. Everyone in Budapest is in danger."

I concede that life is unpredictable, and I thank the Lord that there have been no epidemics of sickness in the home, as it would be hard to find a doctor in the city now. Many of the doctors are Jewish, and they have all been arrested and transported. I am keeping very good health, despite the pressures of our circumstances under occupation.

I am very concerned about Helena* and Margit,* who failed to return to the girls' home after a weekend visit to their families—some are still going home to see their families despite my recommendation that they remain here. I have gone to their homes, both in the Jewish Quarter, but found no one at home. It could be, and I pray that it is, that they have somehow managed to find a way to leave Hungary, perhaps through Romania, or have been issued safe conduct cards by one of the legations and been placed in a safe house somewhere in the city; I know plans were being made to establish these places. In the latter case, I would imagine they could eventually get a message to us about their whereabouts.

It is so hard to know what is going on when all forms of communication are either not working or are under surveillance by the Hungarian police or Nyilas. One virtually has to hand deliver any message now, and even that isn't easy, as police frequently stop, interrogate, and search people in the streets.

Incarceration

Diary of Jane Haining

April 5, 1944

I have been arrested—not officially—but at least forcefully removed from the girls' home and brought to a house in the Buda hills just across the river. I must quickly write the details on a scrap of paper while I have the time, for this is very significant disruption of my up till now predictable, ordered life.

At ten o'clock yesterday morning, while I was working in my office, two Gestapo officers arrived at the door of the mission, knocked once, and then just marched in. I could hear the commotion from upstairs and thought, *How rude of them to enter in such a way!*

The next thing I knew, they were asking for me. Of course, having nothing to fear, I immediately came downstairs to enquire what they wanted. I am not intimidated by these people. Rather, I feel sorry for them, as I know they have little option but to follow orders, even when they don't agree with them. I'm sure many of them would have been kindly family men if it had not been for the war. This war has changed so many people, and not for the better.

I was very surprised by their demand. They gave me only fifteen minutes to pack a bag and be ready to be taken away to who knows where. Fifteen minutes is not long, especially if you don't know where you are going or for how long. I kept calm. I reasoned that I would not be gone long, otherwise I would have been given more instructions about what to bring and more time to pack. So I went upstairs to my room, put on a neat suit, grabbed a few clothes, toiletries, my eye glasses, on which I am now very dependent, and of course some paper and pens, and thrust them into my small overnight bag. The Gestapo men had meanwhile been searching my office. I was distraught at the mess they were making but was certainly not going to let them know that.

I brought my overnight bag downstairs but suddenly realised I had left my Bible behind, so I raced back upstairs to get it. The officers were now searching my room. One of them grabbed the Bible from my hand and threw it on the floor, saying I wouldn't need it where I was going. I could only think that he meant I would not be away long and wouldn't need it, so I left it lying on the floor and returned downstairs. I remembered that the Lord has placed His Word in our hearts, so one night without a Bible would certainly be sustainable.

By this time, quite a number of girls had gathered in the entrance hall of the mission, and several teachers were on the first floor balcony. One of our teachers who lives at the mission, Otti Toth, called out to me in a concerned voice, and I looked up and gave her a smile and a wave. I told the girls that I would be back soon and walked with as much decorum as I could muster, out the door.

The Gestapo officers, following close behind, ushered me into a waiting car. It was a beautiful, sunny, spring day, one of the sort of days you long for after Hungary's cold and grey winter months. As we drove, I noted the lovely daffodils and other spring flowers popping up in window boxes along the city streets and felt at peace. I made up my mind to enjoy this unexpected outing.

I was very curious to see where they would take me. I expected it would be to Gestapo headquarters. My detention had to be a mistake of course—a case of mistaken identity; there were plenty of those in Hungary with so many officials from different agencies trying to do the same job but following different guidelines. Once I arrived at the Gestapo headquarters, I would show them my safe conduct pass, issued by the Swiss Legation, which I had remembered to tuck into my handbag. They would then realise their mistake and release me, hopefully with an apology. Foreigners are still viewed with some level of tolerance here in Hungary.

However, we did not head to the Gestapo building at all, but further down across the river and up into the Buda hills, close to the Swedish Legation. I asked the men where we were going, but they maintained a stony silence. That was when I began to wonder if I had misjudged the whole affair. I tried to hand my captors my safe conduct pass, but they brushed it aside, saying it was valueless.

The car stopped outside a villa that I could only describe as luxurious. This was obviously one of the many properties owned by wealthy Jews, which had been sequestered over the past few days. The owners would have been either arrested or pushed out onto the street with nothing but the clothes on their backs.

A guard opened the tall latticework gate, and we walked inside and up the steps to the house itself. To my surprise, there were no formalities, no questions, and no instructions. I was taken straight upstairs, pushed into the room, in which I now sit, containing a bed, a table, and a chair, and locked in. With nothing to do but to contemplate the dreadfully over-ornate floral wallpaper, or look out the window at a sea of grey and orange-tiled roofs stretching out below the villa towards the river, I decided not to panic or imagine the worst, but to simply meditate on what I knew to be true. As usual, that led me straight back to the Word of God and my favourite scripture.

I couldn't see any hills from my window, as this villa was situated on the hilliest part of the city, but nevertheless I said to myself, over and over:

If I raise my eyes to the hills, from where will my help come?
My help comes from ADONAI, the maker of heaven and earth.
He will not let your foot slip—your guardian is not asleep. No,
the guardian of Isra'el never slumbers or sleeps.

Psalm 121:1-4

Tired from the morning's adventure, I lay down on the lumpy bed and slept for several hours. I was woken by a knock on my door and the key turning. A rather large lady, with a grim face, brought me some soup, bread, and a cup of tea and asked in a rural Hungarian accent whether I needed to go to the bathroom. Of course I leapt at that chance, mostly out of curiosity about this house I was now incarcerated in, and was led down the passageway to a small water closet with a hand basin. The woman stood outside the door until I was finished and then indicated I had to return to my room for my meal. I tried to ask her how long I would be here and when I would see someone from the authorities to clear up this situation, but she just shrugged her shoulders and walked out of the room. The key turned again in the lock. I spent a restless night.

Today has been rainy, adding to the greyness of my situation. I can't help but remember the girls at the home and all the tasks I should have been doing today. I wonder if anyone has been able to get out to the markets this morning. If not, the home will be seriously short of food by tomorrow. I'm also concerned about what the girls have been told about my absence. I certainly don't want them to worry about what must surely be only a temporary absence. I hope Miss Toth and Sophie Victor, another teacher who has a lovely way with the girls, have taken it upon themselves to give them all a special goodnight hug from me.

I can tell there are several others being held in this house, as I have heard muffled conversations and heard others make the short journey to the bathroom. All we need to do is knock on the door and our dour jailer comes to escort us. I am longing to find out who the other inmates are and why they are here. I would also like to know why I am here! I am missing my girls terribly.

Four Days Later

I'm still in this Buda villa with no visits from either interrogators or my friends. Whatever can be happening?

There have been some loud explosions over the past few days, which sound to me like Budapest is being bombed. By whom? I was immediately concerned about my girls and am praying daily that they will not be hurt in any way. Fortunately, today has been quiet.

I have made contact with two other women who say they have been here one month and are expecting to be deported any day. They are both foreigners. They have been told their papers are no longer in order, so they must leave Hungary. It seems the Germans are simply getting rid of anyone they wish to, regardless of the law of the land.

I definitely do not want that to happen to me and will oppose any deportation with all my strength. My job here is not finished.

My girls are currently without their guardian, and I will not willingly leave my post.

I am being well treated, as far as is possible when you have lost your basic right to liberty. I am getting three meals a day, which are sufficiently nutritious. I am allowed into a small lounge for several hours a day and have been given a choice of a few books to read to while away the time.

However, I can get no answers from the staff here about what is to happen to me. I speak both good German and good Hungarian, so they certainly understand my questions, but I get no answers at all.

Every request to be allowed to make contact with the mission is greeted with a gruff shake of the head, and the two letters I wrote and handed to them to deliver, I later found in a rubbish bin in the lounge.

April 12, 1944

Today there has finally been some action but not much! Two Gestapo officers, different ones from those who apprehended me, came to see me. I was asked to step into the lounge and found them sitting at a table, with a bundle of papers in front of them. Shuffling through the papers, they looked up at me, nodded towards a chair for me to sit down, and then went back to studying the papers.

Eventually one of them asked me my name, address, occupation, and nationality.

"My name is Jane Mathison Haining. I'm currently the matron at the Church of Scotland's Scottish Mission to Budapest Girls' Home in Vörösmarty utca. I live on the premises," I answered clearly and confidently. "I'm British but have lived and worked in Budapest for the past decade."

I waited for more questions but was bemused as they simply nodded to the woman orderly who beckoned me and returned me to my room.

I am now sitting down on my bed, and for the first time, downcast in my spirit. What is going on, and why am I here? Why does it take so long for them to process this matter? Why am I not allowed to get a message to the mission? I consider myself to be the most simple of cases. I am a foreigner and therefore not subject to those disastrous Jewish laws. To my knowledge, I have not broken any Hungarian laws. I am not a leader of any subversive organisation or even a member of one. My one aim and goal is to continue my work at the mission, which has always had the full support of the Hungarian government. If only they would tell me what they think I have done, I will be able to set the record straight. If I have been falsely accused, it only requires that I know the accusation, and I will be able to respond confidently and convincingly.

Meanwhile, I return to my only source of sustenance—my faithful Advocate, Friend, and Saviour.

In my beloved Psalms I remember Psalm 42:6(5), "My soul, why are you so downcast? Why are you groaning inside me? Hope in God, since I will praise him again for the salvation that comes from his presence."

Three Days Later

With my freedom so limited, there is little to write about, as each day goes on much as the last.

However, I did have another visit from those two Gestapo officers—they haven't introduced themselves, so I don't know their names. It was much like the first visit except that this time they said there was a delay in dealing with my case because all the information had not yet been gathered. That truly puzzled me as I wondered what information they could possibly need to get.

I had formed a good relationship with the Belgian woman in the room next to mine, swapping information mostly during trips to the bathroom. We were also developing a simple system of communication by knocking quietly on the wall—three knocks meant we should both ask to go to the bathroom, two knocks meant something was amiss, and one knock meant everything is fine. Over time I think we would have refined this system, but unfortunately our knocking must have been too loud. The orderly heard and threatened to put us in rooms at opposite ends of the corridor if we continued. I felt immensely frustrated and humiliated, as if I was a naughty child being told off for a prank!

Oh Lord, how much I have yet to learn about how to live at peace in this new place it has pleased You to set me. I am reminded of the apostles Paul and Silas, who sat in chains in prison singing songs of worship to God (Acts of the Apostles: 16:24-28). Will you, God, bring an earthquake to release me as I worship you? Or is there some purpose that I have not yet discerned for my remaining here?

I am stashing these notes under my mattress so that the orderly doesn't find them, as I'm sure she would remove them if she knew I was keeping a record of my imprisonment. One day, I may get to reread them and smile at the questions I am asking now.

April 20, 1944

Finally something has happened. I have been moved—twice!

The first move was to the basement of the Gestapo Headquarters on Szabadsa Hill, an area I know well from my many summer evening walks with my very good friend Frances Lee. Then, two nights later, I was moved to a room in Hotel Belvedere. I have managed to bring my diary notes with me, secreted in my underwear. I feel a sense of satisfaction that I have succeeded in this act of stealth.

I have been given no reason for the moves but suspect it is to prevent my friends and the mission folk finding me. I'm sure that by now they will be urgently wanting to know where I am. My very good friend, Miss Prém, would immediately think of bringing me a food parcel, and the girls would want to send me notes of encouragement. The only explanation I can think of for their lack of contact is that the Germans are preventing them from knowing where I am. Why would they do that? I have not heard of such secrecy about arrests for anyone but the Jews.

April 24, 1944

My circumstances have changed.

I have not been released but moved to a real prison, the prison on Fö utca, and this time, I am sharing a cell with five other ladies. The best news is that one of them is my good friend, Frances Warburton Lee! She is in prison suspected of espionage, as, it seems, are all the other foreigners here. We hugged each other in amazement when I was led to my cell.

The conditions are very unsavoury here, with an old rusty toilet in the corner of our cell, three sets of bunks with one grey blanket, and a thin pillow on each—no sheets! There are no chairs or tables, and thick bars across the window obscure most of the view of the grey stone building next door. I'm told the food is poor and in short supply. Some days the soup is so watered down, no one can tell what kind of soup it is.

The prison officers took my overnight bag and most of my possessions, allowing me only one set of clothes, one change of underwear, and my toilet bag. Life will be a bit different here. I still have my diary jottings and two small pieces of unused paper. One of my cell mates has a pen. Such little things become extremely important when you are bereft of most of your belongings! Despite all that, I am glad to be here; it is so good to have company. I feel uplifted again in spirit.

The Gestapo has now amassed all the information it wants, and I am now officially arrested on suspicion of espionage for the British. How absurd that is! Any knowledge I have of what is going on politically in Hungary comes from the BBC or from information passed on to the Hungarian Reformed Church by the Nazis themselves.

Interrogation

Diary of Jane Haining

April 30, 1944

Funny how small things become so important when they are in short supply! Suddenly food has taken on a value far beyond my previous experience. I have a new understanding of the verses in the Bible where our precious Lord likened himself to bread!

Jesus says in John 6:48,

> I am the bread which is life. Your fathers ate the man[6] in the desert; they died. But the bread that comes down from heaven is such that a person may eat it and not die. I am the living bread that has come down from heaven; if anyone eats this bread, he will live forever.

Yesterday, Frances was allowed to return under guard to her lodgings to pack up her belongings, so the landlord could rent out the apartment to someone else. She returned with all sorts of treasures, including good things to eat, needle and thread, scissors, a nail file, a brush, and a comb. We all sat down and had a good feed, delighted, like children at a birthday party.

I needed the sustenance, as I had just spent the day at Gestapo Headquarters being interrogated. I shared later with Frances about the ridiculous charges laid against me and laughed a little as I remembered saying, "Guilty," to each in turn, except the last, which I denied vigorously.

The interrogation went something like this:

"Prisoner Haining, be seated." I sat down on a wobbly wooden chair directly in front of my two interrogators' table. One of them had smelly breath and slicked-back hair under his Gestapo uniform hat and slouched uncomfortably in his chair. The other sat forward, elbows on the wooden table, glaring at me with icy blue-grey eyes.

They tossed a paper across the table to me. "You are a political prisoner of the Third Reich." The icy-eyed spokesman paused for effect. "You are accused of the following eight charges. Charge number one: You have been working with the Jews. How do you plead?" These latter words were spat out with unnecessary vehemence.

I smiled a little at the banality of the charge and airily replied, "Guilty as charged. Of course I have been working with the Jews as my work, as matron of the Scottish mission home necessitates that."

"Charge number two: You employed an Aryan as a housekeeper and later dismissed her."

"Guilty again. Of course she came to us of her own free will and had nothing to do with the management of the children, so there was no infringement of the rules. Her job was only to cook and keep house. I was forced to let her go when the law was changed disallowing Aryans to work in a residence where Jews lived. But I found her another position and gave her a generous severance payment, so she was in no way disadvantaged by the change. I believe she felt she was quite generously treated."

That answer prompted a small discussion between my interrogators and a shuffling of the papers before them. They occasionally looked up at me and then back at their papers.

"Charge number three," the spokesman finally barked. "You wept as you sewed the Stars of David on the Jews' clothing, showing an unacceptable degree of empathy."

"Absolutely guilty," I asserted strongly. Now they had my full attention! "My heart went out to these young children branded in such a terrible way."

I couldn't help tears filling my eyes and rolled down my cheeks as I remembered the harsh task I had had to undertake. This must have embarrassed the two interrogators, as they shifted in their chairs and then got up and left the room until I had regained control of my emotions.

On returning to the room, they resumed the performance. "Charge number four: You entertained English visitors!"

"Of course I'm guilty of that. I'm Scottish, so it is entirely natural for me to have British visitors," I said without hesitation. This logical response clearly irritated the two men as they moved quickly onto the next charge with renewed vigour. Both were now sitting forward on their chairs.

"Charge number five: You owned a wireless set and listened to the BBC news."

"Guilty again. A trivial issue, surely, and easily explained. I did have a wireless set, but it was needed so I could hear air raid warnings. It was my responsibility to make sure the girls got safely to the air raid shelter on hearing a warning on the radio."

I was beginning to become annoyed at the ridiculous nature of the charges and somewhat suspicious of their intentions. When they charged me with visiting British prisoners on Count Andrássy's estate in the south of Hungary, I began to feel angry at the injustice of this accusation. I suppose my emotions showed on my normally cheerful face, and they began to watch me like hawks.

"Guilty of the charge as it stands, but it is not a fair representation of the situation," I stated hotly. "The Hungarian Count who owns the property had himself given Dr. Nagy and myself permission to visit these prisoners of war at Christmas time and to hold a Christmas service."

"There is a further serious charge of sending parcels to British prisoners of war," they barked.

"I am definitely guilty of doing that, but it is no crime. The Hungarian government had given permission for these to be delivered," I barked back.

If this was all the Gestapo's weeks of investigation had uncovered, there was little to worry about! But what a waste of energy and of my time!

The final charge, that I had been active in politics, shocked me. It was so ridiculous that I found it hard to respond.

"Not guilty!" I declared emphatically, saying I had never talked about or meddled in politics in my life. This charge would have inspired much mirth among those who knew me.

The Gestapo officers abruptly stood and marched out of the room, and I was left to my musings about this charade.

Actually my worst moment was not during the interrogation, but on the journey back to prison. I was packed with about twelve other women into the back of a small van, which had no windows. It was stiflingly hot, and I had to control myself to not panic as fears of suffocation or being trampled to death crossed my mind. I can honestly say that was the first time I had seriously felt my life to be in danger since my arrest. However, we all arrived safely and were marched back to our respective cells.

Once back in the cell, with a full stomach for the first time in almost a month thanks to Frances's delicious additions to our diet, I sat down to consider further the official paper the Gestapo had given me listing the charges against me.

I smiled. All but one I could not deny and, in any case, would not have wanted to because they were certainly not crimes.

On consideration and after a night's sleep, I feel in no way dismayed by the interrogation. In fact, I am heartened, as they might have accused me of much worse, including my secretarial role for Dr. Nagy's secret meetings and other minor acts of benevolence to the Jews.

The charges are so farcical that I believe even the Gestapo officers will realise they have made a mistake in bringing them. I would expect, to save themselves further embarrassment, they will dismiss my case after a respectable period of time.

May 5, 1944

Today, I received my first parcel from the mission. How wonderful to have my own hairbrush, a change of clothes, and some more paper for writing. I noted my Bible was not among the items in the parcel and know they would have realised how much I would value its inclusion. I can only think it has been lost or removed from the parcel.

We prisoners need always to be on the alert against despondency. Even in our confined circumstances, we must find ways to lift our spirits and not just depend on such random external events as receiving a food parcel or a letter to do it for us.

Frances devised a plan that is working very well. We have started presenting regular concerts with each cell member required to do an item. It is a great relief to have something positive to think about and is helping me to avoid dwelling on my girls and how they are managing at the home without me. I miss them so much.

The night before last, Frances danced a Scottish Reel, which had us all roaring with laughter, especially at the faces she pulled in exercising some of the more difficult moves. Without a gramophone, we had to provide our own music of course, and that was quite a cat's chorus disintegrating into irrepressible giggles as well.

Last night was my turn. Inspired by several parcels of clothing coming for cell mates, I decided we should hold a fashion show, with yours truly as the emcee. I don't know who packs these parcels, but sometimes the most unusual clothing is included, so our fashion show was sure to be entertaining. I did my commentary in German—all those in the cell could understand that language to some degree. It was wonderful to allow our imaginations to soar far above our circumstances as we chuckled over Greta's* red and yellow knickerbockers and Jasmine's* patchwork dress and matching hat.

I am not sure what my next item will be. With such limited resources, I will need to be most innovative.

I should include here some observations about day to day life in jail. For me, this is a unique experience—one which I hope never to have to repeat. As I was told on my arrival, the food is barely sufficient. We live for food parcels.

At present we have a bunk each, which I'm told is exceptional, as sharing bunks is the norm in this prison. We are allowed two baths a week, with two people to a bath. Frances and I have chosen to be bath partners. No one is allowed reading materials, but for some reason, they have not taken Frances's Bible away from her. I truly believe that is God's provision for us.

I have known Frances for about five years now, and never have I seen her so interested in the Word of God. Many times, I had encouraged her to study the Bible, but she had always been so busy and preoccupied with life in general that attending church was the limit of her religious observance.

Now I find it is Frances who every morning reaches for her Bible and beckons me to join her in her morning devotions. What a privilege to share the Word and the presence of God in such surroundings. His Word becomes alive in a way that it never could in normal life circumstances. I have found so many references to imprisonment in the Bible. The meaning of this word is greatly amplified as we read while hunched together on a prison bunk.

My favourite book, the Psalms, continues to uphold and strengthen us. Both Frances and I exclaim each time we find a verse that seems to be speaking directly to us in our circumstances.

Our favourite verse over the past few days has been from Psalm 142:7(6)-8(7).

> Rescue me from my persecutors, for they are too strong for me.
> Lead me out of prison, so that I can give thanks to your name;
> in me the righteous will be crowning themselves, because you
> will have treated me generously.

In the Bible, David prayed this prayer when hiding in a cave, fearing for his life. Stuck in prison and fearing for what the future holds, we are also clinging to this verse and praying that we will both be released.

Our cell mates are beginning to take an interest in this book that brings peace and joy to our hearts and smiles to our faces. Frances has also discovered an ability to pray for others, and it is nothing short of miraculous the way her prayers are being answered. Our cell mates are now coming to her and begging her to pray for their various needs. They say Frances has luck with God!

Oh, thank you, Lord, for providing me with a soul companion with whom to study Your Word and experience your presence in this dark place.

May 11, 1944

We have all been sick. Frances had a terrible tummy bug for four days, and it fell to me to nurse her through it, hoping she had not contracted full-blown dysentery. My greatest concern was that she got enough to drink, as it is so easy to become dehydrated with this illness.

I also fell ill but recovered remarkably quickly, as I have a very strong constitution and am not often troubled by these sicknesses for long.

No sooner was I well than I was called out by the prison officers to go to Gestapo Headquarters for a second interrogation. I put on my best clothes—we all make every effort to be nicely dressed when going for interrogation. I quickly grabbed my handbag, in which was my Swiss safe conduct pass and was hustled out of the cell along the long corridor to the main office and to a waiting car.

We sped through the busy streets, and as I looked out the window I realised I knew nothing about what was happening in Budapest or, in fact, in the war in general. My world had become a microcosm of cell life with the constant interplay of six different personalities, of routine, and of the constant fight against boredom and monotony. Diary, you can see why a journey on the outside, even if it was to an interrogation, was almost something to look forward to.

I couldn't imagine what further charges or questions the Gestapo might have and rather hoped they would tell me that, on investigation, they had decided to withdraw their current charges. I have never heard of this happening, but we are in the strangest of times, so it is very hard to know what might happen next.

The format for the second interrogation was exactly the same as the first. I was ushered into a room where two Gestapo officers sat with their obligatory pile of documents in front of them. After much shuffling of papers, one of the officers repeated all of the charges and asked if I wanted to change any of my responses.

"Not at all," I responded. "I spoke the truth last time, and it is still the truth, so I can change nothing."

One officer left the room after that, and the other took the opportunity to engage me in conversation, asking whether I had any idea who might have denounced me. I was shocked. It hadn't occurred to me that I might have been denounced by someone. My mind went numb for a few seconds, and then I began to wonder who might have had a grudge against me.

Only one person came to mind. It was the young Nyilas member, Schréder, whom I had confronted at the girls' home after he had stayed overnight without permission. Surely not. But then, who else? There was no one else. I am no saint, but I have kept short accounts all my life and have always dealt with any offence, seeking forgiveness or willingly forgiving, as the need arose.

The Gestapo officer eyed me carefully and asked me again who might have denounced me, so I said only one person came to mind and explained what had taken place that morning at the girls' home.

"The only person I can think of is that young Nyilas man, Schréder," I volunteered, more than a little puzzled about where this conversation was going to.

He gave me a strange look and said I might well be right in my assumption, that the charges might well have arisen from this young man and the snippets of gossip he had gleaned from his mother-in-law, the home's housekeeper.

I sensed a degree of empathy, or perhaps even sympathy, in this man.

The second officer re-entered the room, and our conversation was abruptly terminated. We went back to business. The charges were read a second time, and again he demanded to know, this time quite forcefully, whether I wanted to retract any of my statements. I held my ground firmly, repeating that I couldn't change the truth. At that point he turned to me and hissed. "If you love the Jews that much, you deserve what is coming to you!"

This hit me like a thunderbolt. I was supposedly detained on charges of suspected espionage for Britain. Nowhere in the official charges did it make mention of the crime of loving the Jews. Not once had I been questioned on my attitude toward the Jews, only on whether I was working with Jews, which was undeniable. Of course on this last and new charge, I was unquestionably guilty. I would have loved the chance to defend myself on this accusation but was given no such opportunity. As usual, my past actions and my current tears had to speak for me.

My interrogation was finished. I was hustled from the room and placed in a waiting room with a number of other unfortunate prisoners, waiting for the van transport back to prison. Six women were sitting dejectedly on benches as I walked in. No one spoke. Each was absorbed in her own misery or confusion. Others were brought in to join us, and after about three hours, we received orders to file out and into another of those dreadful small vans, where again, like sardines, we survived the short journey back to prison.

145

It was a relief to get back to the safety of my cell. I sat down and told Frances all that had transpired in my interrogation. Between us, we tried to guess why a Gestapo officer would engage me in conversation about the person who denounced me. And especially why he would give me a clue as to the identity of this person. This surely was not usual procedure. The thought crept into my mind that they would not have done that if I was about to be released. I pushed that thought quickly from my mind, not yet ready to consider such an outcome.

On the Move

Diary of Jane Haining

May 13, 1944

Wonderful but short-lived good news! I received my second food parcel from the mission staff yesterday. I shared some lovely pastries with my cell mates—I have no idea where the mission got them from, but they were the most delicious things I have eaten in a long time.

Also in the parcel was some of the ham I cured after finding a great bargain at a market just outside Budapest, days before my arrest. I bought a whole pig there that morning and brought it back to the mission. I managed to make the purchase only because I was first in line and ready as the market opened at five that morning. Oh how long ago that seems!

One may wonder why I would buy pork for a Jewish girls' home, as pork is not exactly kosher,[7] but it was the only meat available, and we were very lucky to be able to get it. I'm sure God will look the other way if any of our Jewish girls wants to eat it. These are extreme circumstances. For those girls who don't want to eat it, there will be of course an extra portion of other food. As you can see, I'm still planning the menu for the home in my mind.

We shared good portions of the ham around in our cell, thoroughly enjoying our first meat in three weeks. Eating it was rather messy. We had to tear it apart with our fingers, as they don't give you knives and forks in prison. However, nothing could detract from our enjoyment of this treat.

I was disappointed to see there was no Bible among the items in the parcel, so I must assume my Bible is lost, destroyed, or confiscated. I just hope the person into whose hands it falls is blessed by it as I have been. After all, God's Word is alive and active, a weapon for His kingdom, so it will be used for His purposes wherever it is.

My hope in this rests on two verses:

> See, the Word of God is alive! It is at work and is sharper than any double-edged sword—it cuts through to where soul meets spirit and joints meet marrow, and it is quick to judge the inner reflections and attitudes of the heart.
>
> Hebrews 4:12

> So is my word that goes out from my mouth – it will not return to me unfulfilled; but it will accomplish what I intend, and cause to succeed what I sent it to do.
>
> Isaiah 55:11

Now for my other news—today, in fact at five in the morning, the prison guards came to our cell door and called my name. "Haining!" They try to be as impersonal as possible, and we are now reduced to surnames only. Everyone scrambled up, alarmed at this unexpected event. Surely I wasn't being called at five in the morning for another interrogation?

I was told to get my belongings together as I was being moved to a camp, so I hastily grabbed a change of clothes, my handbag with my Swiss safe conduct pass, which I still carry in case one day someone cares to take notice of it, my eyeglasses, and my toiletries. I forgot my hairbrush, which I now realise I left to dry on the small windowsill in the cell. I have given most of the clothing sent to me in parcels from the mission to other cell mates who have very few clothes and need something respectable to wear when they are called up for Gestapo interrogations, so my possessions are few.

I fished my precious diary notes out from under my mattress and hastily passed them on to Frances, saying I didn't know what was ahead of me, but I felt they would be safer with her. She could return them to me after the war.

She took them and assured me she would guard them with her life, at which we both laughed. Then she and the other cellers, as we had begun to call ourselves, wished me the very best, saying they were very jealous that I was being taken to a work camp where the conditions would certainly be better than this dark and dingy prison.

Frances asked me to pray for them all when I was out each day experiencing the precious sunshine and fresh air and to remember our special verse that David of the Bible prayed when he was hiding in a cave, especially the part that said, "Lead me out of prison, so I can give thanks to your name" (Psalms 142 8(7)). I'm sure Frances thought God had answered this prayer for me, as I was being released into a more agreeable place while she and the other cellers had to remain. Dear Frances! I left that place with their blessings still ringing in my ears, but little did they, or I, know the truth.

As I walked out the door, Frances thrust a strip of ham into my hand, the remains of yesterday's feast, saying I might need it.

I was bundled into a waiting van by prison staff and taken to the train station. By now, I had accepted intellectually that God was not going to release me just yet; I was just off to another form of imprisonment. But emotionally, I was grieving for my work with girls at the home, always concerned that I could not be there to protect them at this crucial time. That was so frustrating! Everything was bearable, except that.

All the camps were outside Budapest in the countryside, so I knew I would soon be further away from my girls.

The sight at the train station astounded me. Gestapo guards, some with vicious-looking dogs, were rounding up a huge sea of women and children on the platform to which I was led. Goodness knows where they came from. Some were crying, some screaming for children that had somehow become separated from them. Others had stony faces, showing no emotion at all. They looked like dead women walking. Many carried no bag, and some had only summer clothes and slippers, as if they had been plucked from their kitchens without warning. I felt very overdressed with my warm jacket and sturdy shoes.

I glanced across at the platforms opposite and saw people going about their everyday business, catching early trains to work, and wondered how they could continue their lives as usual with this grotesque scene just a few metres away. Whatever were they thinking?

"Prisoner Haining," barked a guard. He grabbed my arm and yanked. He checked me off on a master list held be a Gestapo officer.

"Yes," I gasped.

"Get in line." I was unceremoniously propelled forward and found myself squashed into a huddle of women being lined up to climb aboard cattle truck number ten on the waiting train. I asked the woman in front of me, who seem relatively composed, if she knew where the train would take us. She gave a sad smile and said we were bound for Kistarcsa Transit Camp, just twenty-five kilometres away. Farther than that she didn't know. I was very glad it wasn't farther away as I noted the line of women due to travel in my carriage was getting longer by the minute.

Eventually, we were all squeezed on board. I was amazed at how many women were forced onto my truck. There were no seats, so we were all standing. Personal space was a thing of the past with each woman squashed against the next, ribs and elbows digging into the next person if anyone so much as attempted to shift position. The fear I had felt in the prison van returned, so I closed my eyes and prayed for strength from my Saviour who never slumbers nor sleeps.

At the end of our journey, we all piled out onto the station platform. We were ordered to form rows, five across, and began the march through the back streets of the town to the nearby camp. Women with small children had to pick the little ones up, as we were required to keep up a brisk pace with dogs barking at our heels as though we were a flock of sheep. The woman next to me had two small children under three years old, so I carried the older of the two. Both children were immobilised through fear, not a sound escaping their lips. How traumatic for these little ones. It was quite bad enough for us adults, who could at least understand something of what was going on.

I noticed that many of the women in this human sea of misery were Roma (Gypsies) or other races. I wondered what had transpired to bring them to this point. No doubt they were also wondering how a short, blonde (now greyish) haired Scottish woman, still with a strong Scottish brogue had managed to get entangled in this web.

At the camp we were lined up on the parade ground. Our names were called, and we were assigned to barracks. We were told this was a holding camp for political prisoners while their final destinations were decided. I couldn't help wondering just how this German war machine could justify labelling toddlers and babies political prisoners, even if they had any justification at all in labelling their mothers so.

Once in my barracks and having found a space on a bunk—we were sleeping three across a bunk—I brought out the small roll of toilet paper I had managed to uplift from the prison, and the stubby pencil I had been given by one of my cellers and set about recording the day's events.

From now on, it may be harder to keep up my diary unless the Red Cross is notified of my whereabouts and is allowed to send me a parcel. I had never dreamed that my shorthand skills would be so useful and for such an unusual purpose. With shorthand, much information can be recorded in a very small space, and with my own personal version of it, it will be difficult for anyone else to translate. I feel relatively safe, even in this transit camp, in keeping a diary in this format.

Later

After a long day of train travel and forced march, many of the women lay down on their bunks, too confused and disconsolate to talk or investigate their surroundings. I put my latest diary notes under my side of the bunk before going outside to have a look around. To be sure, I was out in the fresh air for the first time in many weeks, but a ten-foot-high wire fence with barbed wire on top surrounding the camp was a strong reminder of my prisoner status.

As I pondered my condition and asked the Lord to show me what was happening and how this could be part of His will for me, verses from another Psalm popped into my mind. How glad I am that I had memorised so many of the Psalms and reinforced my memories as I taught them to the girls at the home!

I repeated to myself over and over as I walked, Psalm 141:8-10:

> For my eyes, ADONAI,[8] Adonai,[9] are on you; in you I take refuge; don't pour out my life. Keep me from the trap they have set for me, from the snares of the evildoers. Let the wicked fall into their own nets, while I pass by in safety.

As I walked I repeated time and again, "Don't pour out my life, Lord, don't pour out my life."

Now, back in the barracks, I am meditating on what transpired as I walked around the camp.

I have taken a step into unknown (to me) territory. Emotionally, I have come to the footstool of the Lord in a new way. Emotionally, I am finally facing my future, the future that I still don't understand. I am allowing myself to think thoughts that I have previously never dared to consider. What if it is God's will for me to remain here, or worse, to be sent on to one of the concentration camps we have heard such disquieting rumours about? I am, after all, in a transit camp, which means I will transit to somewhere. So, despite all, I am now pleading with the Lord that it not be so.

I cannot forget how Jesus, my dear Saviour, pleaded in the garden of Gethsemane that the cup of the cross be removed from Him. But ultimately, he said, "Not my will, but Yours, Father God."

Could I ever submit like that to my God's will? Do I have it in me to make such a sacrifice? How could I find such courage and faith when I still don't understand what purpose such a sacrifice might serve? Am I departing dangerously from my usually rational and practical view of life, or am I moving closer to the truth about faith and life itself?

Whatever the answers to these questions (I am still hoping one day I will reread this with the answers already at hand), I continue to beg of my Saviour, "Don't pour out my life!"

A Life Poured Out

Diary of Jane Haining

May 20, 1944

Though I lack the stamina to do this, I feel I must make at least a short entry in my diary. I still have some toilet paper, and I managed to smuggle my pencil through a detailed body search by simply dropping it beforehand and scooping it up afterwards as I returned to my place in the line.

In Fö utca Prison, I was reduced to a surname. I am now reduced to a number—79467.

How can I ever describe what I have just been through? I don't know any words to fully express the misery and human degradation I have witnessed over the past five days.

On May 15, my name was called at the transit camp, and I and about ninety Hungarian women were ordered to collect our possessions and present ourselves at the main marshalling area. We were being relocated to better surroundings they said, where we would have the opportunity to work for the German state and for the benefit of our own souls! We could bring whatever we owned, and to be sure, our possessions would be accommodated on our transport.

The group was mostly Jewish but with quite a number of others. I couldn't see another British person or even Western European amongst them, however. All were eager to go, and those left behind

155

murmured that it was unfair that these lucky ones got to move on so quickly to their new work camp.

I felt the warmth of the Lord's arms around me, as I have so often felt as I stepped out onto dangerous ground. But despite this, I was not prepared for what was to come.

We walked, again in formation, to the train station. Again the dogs and guards were there, shouting and waving batons at us. But this time they actually struck those who couldn't keep up the pace.

Fear gripped the group, and one or two women actually tried to break away and flee into the deserted streets of the town. Snarling dogs soon brought them back into line. I lifted my eyes to the Lord, from whence comes my help, and kept pace with the group.

Again, railway cattle trucks were drawn up at the platform, and again we were squashed in with standing room only. I cannot fully share, even with you, diary, the nightmare of the next four days. May it suffice to say we travelled slowly, with many stops, for the whole of those four days without any relief, without room to sit down, and without even room to turn around. We stood, eventually falling asleep on our feet, held up by the bodies around us. Several women near me began to feel unwell; one vomited continuously, and another had what I think must have been a heart attack and died. No one could come to her aid. There were no toilet stops, so we all had to relieve ourselves as we stood, praying silently that this nightmare would soon be over.

The worst thing of all was the thirst that gripped us. Several people had tin mugs which they managed to pass to those pressed against the outer walls of the truck. When we stopped at one station we heard voices close to the truck and those with mugs pushed them through small openings high in the wall, begging for water.

"Please, please, water, any water. We're desperate. We're dying of thirst," they croaked.

Someone outside must have heard and understood, and a hose was soon aimed at our carriage. Some water filled the extended cups, but most simply sprinkled through and onto the seething mass of humanity inside, wetting us and adding further to our discomfort. An angry shout in German told us the hose sprayer had been discovered and his act of charity instantly terminated.

Now wearing wet clothes, we began to shiver uncontrollably as the evening temperatures dropped. Only the smallest amount of water in the mugs ever reached human lips, most spilling as the train jolted into movement again. A deep despondency engulfed us. Each human soul reached into itself and found only darkness and emptiness. There were no more complaints, no more murmurings; only a dreadful resignation. The encouraging words of the German guards at the transit camp rang hollow in our ears, increasing the pain of our souls. And so it went on, interminably, for day after day.

At our destination, the guards unlocked our cattle truck, and we finally poured out onto a long ramp. We were surprised to see we were not at a train station, but inside a camp. A quick look around confirmed this was no summer holiday camp. Guards with guns, batons, and dogs were everywhere. Prisoners in ill-fitting striped uniforms skulked around the edges of the scene, shoulders stooped and barely raising their eyes from the ground.

"*Raus, raus!*" the guards continued to scream at us.

We were marshalled on the ramp into a long line; each woman who had been able to keep in contact with her luggage still clutched her own suitcase, bag, or coat. The bodies of the dead were unceremoniously dumped to one side.

Once we were all in line, the camp commandant welcomed us warmly and announced that we were now inmates of Auschwitz Birkenau Work Camp. He apologised profusely for the conditions under which we had travelled to the camp and said he would instigate an inquiry immediately into why the service had been so sub-standard.

We were then told that we would shortly be divided into two groups—those who were fit and ready for work, and those who needed some rest and relaxation to gain strength before being allotted a work detail. Women were not to fear if they found themselves separated from their children at this point, as they would be reunited by the end of the day, once the children had been given a medical check by a doctor. The group calmed down considerably at these words; desperate women hoped that the nightmare was finally over.

Perhaps privy to more information than most of the women in the group, I was not so easily convinced. I watched carefully as the line inched forward, noting that mothers with babies, children, pregnant women, the old and the ill were all assigned to a new line on the left, while the young and fit were directed to the right. Just ahead of me a very fit-looking woman of only about twenty-five years of age was directed to the left-hand group. She was wearing eyeglasses.

I felt a quiet voice warning me to remove my glasses, so I hastily pushed them into my jacket pocket, pulled myself up to my full (short) stature and strode briskly forward. As I approached the selection point, I found myself directed to the right. A huge relief flooded me—I didn't know why.

The left-hand line was marched off in one direction while we were directed to a complex in another, where we were told we would have a medical examination, our heads would be shaved for reasons of hygiene, we would have a shower, and we would be given our camp uniforms.

Stripped naked, lines of women filed past the doctor and through a mass shower, and were then asked to hand their clothes and other possessions in to a large dour *fräulein* for safekeeping before receiving uniforms. I slipped my eyeglasses and pencil out of my jacket pocket before handing it to the woman and deposited them in the pocket of the flimsy striped garment, which was to be my camp uniform. We then lined up to have our heads shaved.

Our clothes, watches, any jewellery, and other possessions were placed carefully in individual numbered containers and whisked away. We were directed through another door and asked to sit in a waiting room. Through a doorway we could hear gasps and shrieks, and my blood turned to ice. My mind went instantly to the only source left for strength.

Psalm 27:1 says "ADONAI is my light and my salvation; whom do I need to fear? ADONAI is the stronghold of my life; of whom should I be afraid?"

I repeated this scripture several times, finding that hearing myself say it aloud increased its power to calm my nerves. Several women sitting near me looked sideways at me, puzzled. I rather think they wondered if I had lost control of my mind!

Women were being directed through the door in front of us but obviously exiting somewhere else. It was now my turn, and I stood up when beckoned and passed through the doorway. Without my eyeglasses on, my vision was not good, but I could see a long line of chairs with women prisoners sitting on them; at each, a white-coated person was carrying out some sort of procedure on their arms. I sat where indicated and realised we were being branded like cattle. I closed my eyes, waited for the sharp sting of the stylus on my skin, refusing to make any sound of discomfort.

The procedure was finished, and when I opened my eyes, I had been reduced to a number, branded with indelible dye on my right wrist.

I was pushed from the chair and ushered out another door, given a glass of water and herded with a group of about ten other women to our barracks. As the door was opened, we recoiled, repulsed by the smell of urine and other unpleasant human odours. The guards barked at us to enter, find a space on a bunk, and rest until called for work. We crept into the dark barracks, found spaces, and lay our desperately tired bodies down, most of us falling into a deep sleep.

I was wakened a short time later—I no longer had my watch, so I couldn't tell how long—by the sting in my right wrist. It was swelling and looking ugly and red. I put on my eyeglasses to inspect the damage. Other new arrivals were also feeling the discomfort.

I reached for my pencil to record the events of the past four days. My desire to record these unthinkable injustices is outweighing any discomfort I feel. Does the world know what is going on in these camps? Most of those I have left behind in Budapest certainly don't.

May 30, 1944

At dusk on our first day at Auschwitz-Birkenau, the rest of the occupants of my barracks arrived back from their work places. Plied with questions by the ten of us who were newcomers to the barracks, they told us bluntly and without emotion that the other line of women and children from our train had gone directly to their deaths in the camp's huge gas chambers, and their bodies were burnt in a crematorium nearby.

"They've gone up the chimney," they said without a hint of emotion. These women were experienced camp inmates, those who have been here more than one month. Few of us believed what they were saying—it was too grotesque. We thought their minds had been deranged by the terrible circumstances.

They described their work conditions in local factories and inside the camp. I couldn't believe it when they said those who had gone up the chimney were the lucky ones. They warned us not to get sick, and if we did, to never allow the guards to know, as we would be sent to the infirmary where infections of all kinds raged and guards regularly selected the worst cases to be gassed or shot.

"And be careful you don't get behind in your work," offered one skeleton of a woman who spoke good German and was probably about twenty-five but looked closer to fifty. "If you are too weak and can't keep up, or if you get sick, you'll be sent off to barracks twenty-five! No one has ever returned from there!"

And finally, anyone found disobeying any rules would be instantly selected for the firing squad or public gallows.

This was a cruel introduction to the next stage on my journey. The Lord kept whispering in my ear: "My peace I give you. My peace I give you."

I soon learned that I had been classified as a political prisoner but somehow had been placed in the Jewish women's barracks. These women all had the Star of David tattooed on their arms alongside their number. I pondered this anomaly for several days until one night when, unable to sleep for the wails and moans of my distraught barracks companions, revelation came.

I remembered the words of the Gestapo officer in my second interrogation in Budapest and his contorted face as he sneered that if I loved the Jews that much, I deserved what was coming to me.

It finally occurred to me that I was being held, not for allegedly spying for Britain, but for my work with the Jewish girls and their community in Budapest—now I was sharing their fate! My fate had been determined from the start.

My soul was troubled beyond measure. I begged the Lord for some insight into how this could be and what His purpose was in my circumstances.

Ever faithful, the Lord came back to me in my hour of darkness, with a scripture that brought the first ray of real light and understanding in weeks into my wretched soul.

He spoke these words to me from Isaiah 40:1,9:

> 1: Comfort and keep comforting my people," says your God. "Tell Yerushalayim[10] to take heart..." 9: You who bring good news to Tziyon,[11] get yourself up on a high mountain; you who bring good news to Yerushalayim, cry out at the top of your voice! Don't be afraid to shout out loud! Say to the cities of Y'hudah,[12] "Here is your God!"

My mind raced back to those carefree days in my little Scottish village of Dunscore, when I climbed up into the craggy, heather-coated hills and found my God there.

With my mind renewed and my spirit lifted, I found myself unbelievably floating above my circumstances. I felt the presence of angels around me, the warmth of their immediate presence. This was nothing less than a miracle.

Diary, everything has changed. I now have a job to do, an important job that only I can do. And as the women from my barracks are disappearing in twos and threes almost daily, presumably to barracks twenty-five, I can see the mission is urgent.

June 5, 1944

Most of our barracks has been assigned work in a huge warehouse within the camp, where clothes and personal possessions of all types are sorted and packed for transportation from here in southern Poland to Germany. We call this warehouse Canada, as it reminds us all of the country we imagine farthest away from Auschwitz and from our suffering. The work is hard, back-breaking, with very long hours.

Every day someone falls ill or simply collapses from exhaustion or lack of nutrition. These workers are brought back to the barracks and given a postcard to write to their family or whomever they choose, which must be written in pencil and in German (for censorship purposes). They are allowed only to express how well they are being treated, ask for some items of food or a Red Cross parcel to be sent, as would be normal in an ordinary prison, and some personal detail so those back home know the card is authentic. The cards are collected, and then the women are marched off. The experienced inmates shake their heads after each departure and pronounce only three words on the fate of these women—"Up the chimney!"

There is little else to talk about here. The women discuss the day's work and how hard it has been, who has been removed from the barracks, or the latest hangings, shootings, or floggings.

Yesterday, I engaged a young Jewish woman in conversation about the hereafter and what she might expect. Considering that death is at the forefront of the mind of every prisoner in this camp, the hereafter must surely be a topic worthy of thought!

I was amazed and concerned to find she had still not considered the possibility of meeting her Maker, nor the identity of her Messiah. She suggested she would decide about this when the time came, when the Messiah returned to the earth, as spoken of by the prophets. I felt reasonably sure she was not going to have the privilege of waiting to make this choice, so I gently shared with her what her Scriptures revealed about her Messiah and her Maker. She was dumbfounded and wanted to hear more.

I am taking every opportunity now to talk to those who will listen, to tell them their God is here, with them, asking them just to lift their eyes to Him in their misery. I tell them how the Scriptures have transported me to another level where the trials I am going through cannot destroy my spirit. Some are listening; some are not. But there is a new atmosphere in our barracks. You could almost call it peaceful.

June 7, 1944

My God, you have rescued me—but only in the nick of time! This afternoon I had an accident at work, tripping over a shoe that had fallen from a box packed for shipment. I twisted my ankle, which immediately became swollen.

I attempted to get to my feet before the guards noticed but was spotted by an eagle-eyed woman who screamed at me to get up and come to her. Terrified, I hobbled over to her, and of course, she noticed the swelling. She called for another guard, who grabbed me roughly by the arm and marched me back to my barracks. I assured him my ankle was not badly injured and I would be available for work the next day. I sat on my bunk and wept.

This evening, our elected barracks leader came to me and apologetically handed me a postcard, saying that I knew what to do with it and to pass it back to her when I had written what was necessary. I chose to send my last words, for indeed it seemed that these might well be so, to Miss Prém, my dear friend and colleague at the mission. I completed the card and waited to be called out from the barracks.

At nine o'clock this evening, the guard came, calling me and two other women out. The eyes of the rest of the women were downcast as they always were when women were being removed from the barracks. No one wanted to look death in the face. We stood up shakily (my ankle was still very sore) and walked outside. The guards checked the numbers on our wrists against a list and then a discussion arose. They looked again at my wrist and shook their heads.

My German was fluent enough to follow their conversation.

"This one doesn't have the star," one said. "Look. Can she be sent on to twenty-five?"

"We'd better be careful about that one," another responded. "She could be a special case, one of the plants. Better leave her behind."

I gather they thought I was a prisoner spy of some sort, placed there to observe the barracks inmates.

Hugely relieved, I went back inside the barracks and was greeted by eighty sets of eyes bulging in surprise. One woman whispered that Jane's God was protecting her!

I now had the attention of every prisoner in my barracks. They began to discuss why I was placed with them and whether I was a barracks spy. I told them the story of my work in Budapest and of my arrest. There was a long silence as I finished my story, and then one woman began to weep, saying "You did this for us!" "No," I answered, "I don't understand how it came to this, but my God did this for you! He has brought me here to show you how much He cares for you."

July 17, 1944

My heart is so heavy, but a strange peace is enfolding me. Diary, something tells me this may be my last entry. I am asking a dear woman in one of the political prisoner barracks to guard these last jottings.

Today again there was an unfortunate incident in the warehouse. This time, I was sent back to the barracks because of my poor eyesight, which I had managed to conceal until now.

I had been given a new job, checking off boxes of children's toys on a list ready for transportation. The job made me weep almost as much as sewing the Stars of David onto my girls' coats at the mission had done, because I knew these toys had belonged to the innocent and precious little children who had ended their lives in the terrible gas chambers in this camp. Through my tears I was quite unable to read the sets of figures on the list. In a moment of forgetfulness, I drew my eyeglasses out of my pocket and put them on.

Instantly, Borysko*, the most draconian guard of all in the warehouse, renowned for his cruelty, spotted my action and screamed for me to step aside. Again I was unceremoniously bundled back to the barracks to await my fate.

Another postcard, another message. Again I have addressed it to Miss Prém. I hope she received my last post card, as I have had no answer, but just in case, I have repeated some details...

I hear the clomp of heavy boots. The guard has just come for me...it is Borysko.

A Futile Hope

Diary of Jane Haining

Miss Prém's Notes—April 14, 1944

I have decided to add a little to my dear Jane's diary, which she passed to me shortly before being taken away by the Gestapo so that she will still have a full record of events here at the mission.

We have all been suffering huge anguish since she was taken, made altogether worse by the lack of information about her whereabouts. All of us have made the greatest efforts to find her. Bishop Ravasz, head of the Hungarian Reformed Church, approached our Hungarian premier, Dome Sztojay. He took with him Nicholas Mester, state counsellor at the Ministry of Education, and apparently, secretly, also a leading figure in organising the activities of the underground nationalist resistance movement. I am unclear as to why Mr. Mester, of all people, became involved in this situation. As far as I know, Jane has had no dealings with any underground resistance movement. Is the government, once so pro-Germany, now sympathetic to those groups? One is most unlikely to get answers to these questions from anyone who actually knows what is going on.

Hungarian regent, Admiral Horthy, was apparently livid when he heard that Jane had been apprehended. He, the Swiss Consul, and Bishop Ravasz then approached the Hungarian authorities, asking for her release. Mr. Horthy went so far as to order the Minister of

Foreign Affairs to get her released immediately. I understand the bishop even offered to guarantee Jane's retention as a prisoner in the church's deaconess' home.

All has been to no avail. Not only was the Hungarian government powerless to act because any petition from the Hungarian government fell on deaf, German ears, but they were also unable to find out where she was being held. This is unprecedented treatment for a foreigner in Hungary and is of grave concern to us.

As a last resort, we are organising teams of people from the Reformed Church and the mission to go from prison to prison, asking whether Jane might be incarcerated there, and if so, for permission to bring her a food parcel.

Miss Prém's Notes—April 26, 1944

Finally, we have found her! It was quite by chance. This morning, two of the mission staff decided to visit the Fö utca Prison, despite that prison usually being reserved for criminals, and the administration officer at the prison was in a good enough mood to check through his list. He found her name—there she was, in cell number twelve.

It appears there are a number of foreign prisoners there now, categorised as political prisoners and possibly awaiting deportation. If I know Jane at all, she will fight deportation to her last breath. Her passion for the mission and the girls she looks after is something to behold.

We have gained permission from the prison to deliver a food parcel each week. That is the maximum they will allow. So we will make it as big as possible. I think food will be a priority, and of course her beloved Bible, if we can find it. Her room was left in a dreadful mess, and I'm not sure what the Gestapo officers left, what they destroyed, and what they took away with them.

Now that she has been located, perhaps Reverend Lajos Nagy and Bishop Ravasz will have more of a chance of obtaining her release. I do hope this will happen soon, as it is getting more and more difficult to answer the girls' questions about their beloved Miss Haining. Some of the little ones are crying themselves to sleep because they miss their goodnight hugs; the older girls seem to have gone into themselves, which perhaps is a more unhealthy form of grief. No one talks about her, but everyone thinks about her. These are indeed dark days at the mission.

Miss Prém's Notes—April 29, 1944

We have managed to deliver one food parcel to Jane. We put in as much food as we could, her hair brush, which I know she would have missed, some clean clothing, paper and pencils, and several books. Her Bible we couldn't find. The prison administrator took the parcel and said it would be searched, and whatever was permissible would be passed on to her.

Sophie Victor and Reverend Nagy took the parcel, but despite their pleas, they were not allowed to speak to Jane. They were told she was in good health.

Miss Prém's Notes—May 6, 1944

Again I am drawn to add to dear Jane's diary.

We still have had no contact with Jane and no information on the charges against her, although we have heard from the prison authorities that charges have been laid. This is very frustrating, but there is little we can do but wait.

Meanwhile, things are changing rapidly here at the mission and in Hungary in general. Many of us are very concerned about the rounding up of the Jews from the Hungarian countryside into village ghettos at the behest of the Germans. They are using Hungarian troops to do this dirty work. The Jews are being put to work in local factories or sent off to work camps, and I have heard their working and living conditions are dreadful. Many are becoming sick and dying. There are no Jews left in the countryside.

Fortunately, this has not happened in Budapest—not yet. The city Jews are more aware of what is going on and will try their best to avoid any such mobilisation, I think. However, they are being asked to live in designated Jewish houses, and the Hungarian residents of these houses are being forced to move out. I do not like the sound of this initiative, as it makes the Jews more vulnerable to the Nyilas' campaign of terror against them.

I don't know what will happen to the boarders at the girls' home, as I fear they will also be required at some point to move into these Jewish houses. We will do our best to obstruct such a move.

There is talk of the Association of Christian Jews taking over the third floor of the mission as their headquarters. But there is also a rumour that the mission may be used as a refuge for Jewish mothers and children under the auspices of the Swedish Red Cross, if things deteriorate further.

In that regard, the Swedish businessman Raoul Wallenberg, who is now the First Secretary at the Swedish Legation in Budapest, has been a tower of strength, organising Swedish passports for any Jew who wants one. He is looking at ways to hide the Jews until they can be transported to safety outside Hungary. There are many others trying to do the same thing as concern grows for their safety. Many Jews have Christian friends who are doing their best to shelter them, but at the risk of being found out by the Gestapo, or almost worse, by the Nyilas, and being arrested and transported to work camps.

It is hard to know what to do for the best to protect the girls in these circumstances.

Miss Prém's Notes—August 23, 1944

A final addition to the diary of a truly courageous woman, one for whom I have the utmost admiration and for whom I am grieving without solace.

We attempted to take another food parcel to Jane at the Fö utca Prison in early May, only to find she was no longer there.

Frantic enquiries at all the prisons in Budapest produced no results, nor did the urgent requests by Reverend Nagy and the Hungarian Reformed Church to the German authorities, asking them to divulge her whereabouts.

We worried day and night about her, praying that she would be safe.

Then I received a postcard from her, postmarked Auschwitz. Our hearts sank even lower, and our prayers became more fervent. We notified the British authorities and attempted to reply to the postcard but have no idea if our reply was delivered.

A second postcard, this one more of a letter, did not arrive until after the Jewish Mission Committee had been notified officially on August 2, by the British Under-Secretary, that Jane had been imprisoned in Auschwitz. Urgent representations were made to the British Foreign Office and to the British Red Cross to do all they could to secure her release. Reverend Nagy also sent food parcels to Auschwitz for her.

The letter[13] read as follows (translated from German):

Auschwitz, 15 July, 1944

My dearest Margit,

I have not yet had an answer to my first letter, but I know that it's not your fault. I'll repeat briefly, in case by chance you hadn't received it. You may write to me twice a month and I may write to you once a month, only.

Parcels are not restricted in number, nor in regard to names (of the recipients). I asked you to give my name to the Red Cross but also to send me a few parcels until the Red Cross can begin (sending me things), but in addition, if possible, I should always like to receive from you apples or other fresh fruit and biscuits, rusks, bread-stuffs of that kind, because of course the Red Cross doesn't send things like that.

Margit, what are you thinking of doing with the flour? Are you going to sell it? What is upstairs is the best of[14] but you know, ought one to sift through all that is left? Have you used up the eggs too?

How are you all? I think of you day and night lovingly and longingly. I'm waiting for news of what everyone is doing, including your dear family, Margit. Is the old aunt still alive?

There's not much to tell about what is going on here. There are mountains on the horizon (?) here too, further away (or wider) than ours to be sure, but still! Now I send appropriate greetings to the whole family and kiss and embrace you.

Your loving Jean."

On August 17, we received a call from the Swiss Legation here in Budapest saying they had notification of Jane's death and that the German Legation held her death certificate. This stated Jane, "who was arrested on justifiable suspicion of espionage against Germany, died in hospital in Auschwitz on July 17, of cachexia, following intestinal catarrh."[15]

This news deeply saddened all at the mission, and the remaining girls were inconsolable. The mission staff was already well aware that Auschwitz was a camp from which few would return, but that our dear matron had suffered some dreadful fate there was unthinkable. We did not believe the information on the death certificate, as we knew our Jane well and could not see her succumbing so quickly to some new and serious medical problem.

We have poured over the contents of her last letter many times, and I personally do not see it as the letter of a desperately ill person. In fact, I would fit that description at this point, not our Jane. I think she was trying to get a message past the censors to us.

I could not imagine her enquiring of one of my aunts, whom she did not know well, and her references to upstairs and to the mountains seem to refer obliquely to the hereafter. There are no mountains around Budapest, only small hills. I believe Jane was talking of that heavenly mountain, Mount Zion—to Jane, mountains had always represented a place to meet God. So I'm inclined to think Jane was warning us of her imminent death.

Yesterday we saw the final act in the story of a life poured out for others. A Gestapo officer appeared at the door of the mission with a bundle of Jane's personal belongings and her official death certificate. As if delivering a bunch of flowers, the young man casually handed us the small container of precious memories... and my heart broke.

The Final Word

Fittingly, the final word goes to a former boarder at the girls' home, who made the following anonymous contribution to a commemorative gathering for Jane Haining at an Advent service at St. Columba's Church in Budapest, in 1985. Phrases in parenthesis added by the author to give correct context to this abbreviated testimony:

> I'm not worthy to stand here (at the commemorative gathering) but I think there is no one else who owes so much to the Scottish Mission as I.

> After my father's death, I was eleven years old and in very poor health. There was little hope for my survival. I was brought to the Scottish Mission and Miss Haining accepted me on a fellowship basis. What others brought from home, I had to learn from the Scottish School—how to dress, to behave, to understand people, to work, to enjoy life. Here, I learned to love, to pray, to believe, and distinguish between good and evil.

> Miss Haining never preached at us; she just flashed her eyes and said a word or two. For instance, one well-to-do inmate haughtily showed us her expensive clothes. Miss Haining watched her for a while and asked sharply, "Why do you show off with your father's money? Where is your own achievement?

Aren't you ashamed of yourself?" It was Miss Haining that told me the bitter truth (about my origins). I was born a Jewess and the parents I knew had only adopted me. Thus, I must feel very much obliged to my (adoptive) mother.

Thirty years later (after a holiday) I was reluctant to return and had decided to leave my eighty-two year old mother for good. But Miss Haining appeared in a dream to me and asked me once again, "Aren't you ashamed of yourself?" What was her secret, how could she reach people so effectively? It was genuine living love...she could have chosen security (she could have returned to her home before Hungary entered the war, and after the German occupation she was invited to find refuge in some embassies), but she knew she must stay with her flock. She died at the same place and in the same way as (some of) her children did. She followed Christ's example to the very end.

Postscript

Nicholas Railton, in his book *Jane Haining and the Work of the Scottish Mission with Hungarian Jews, 1932 – 1945,* (page 73) states that Reverend George Knight returned to Hungary in 1946 to express to the chief rabbi of the Budapest Jewish community, the Church of Scotland's grief at the suffering of the Jewish people....

> The Church of Scotland, despite being on record as condemning anti-Semitism and racism, also called on its members to confess that it too had a share in the miseries and plight suffered by the Jewish nation. This contrite, humble approach in the immediate post-war world opened doors and paved the way to better relations with the Jewish community. This was particularly true in the case of Hungary, where anti-Semitism survived the war.

In April, 2010, Hungary held national elections. Prior to the election, London's *The Times* newspaper reported (April 11, 2010) that Hungarian caretaker prime minister, Gordon Bajnai, warned that the "monster" (political party Jobbik) was at the door and threatening to crush Hungarian democracy. Various other media reports commented on the eerily similar appearance of the Jobbik banner to the banner used by the pro-Nazi Hungarian Arrow Cross Party (Nyilas), which gained power in 1944 in Hungary. Arrow Cross committed untold atrocities against minority groups, particularly the Roma people (Gypsies) and Jews, such as the massacre of Jews on the banks of the River Duna (Danube). An iconic memorial of metal shoes on the river bank, visited by many tourists, commemorates this sad event.

The following report was published in The Times on April 20, 2010:

> A far-right party, whose candidates have voiced anti-Semitic and anti-Gypsy rhetoric, was on course for a breakthrough in Hungarian elections amid predictions that it would finish third, just behind the governing socialists. Jobbik, which maintains a uniformed wing that marches in military formation, was set last night to win its first parliamentary seats against a backdrop of anti-government resentment and economic downturn. ... Jobbik... draws much of its support from the young and is strong in many universities. It has a slick, multinational internet presence and has sidestepped the traditional political establishments and the mass media.

In the previous parliament, Jobbik, which has described itself as radically nationalistic, had no seats, but in the 2010 elections, it gained forty-seven seats—16.7 percent of the 263-seat parliament. As predicted by The Times, it became the third largest party in a parliament dominated post-election by the centre-right Fidesz Party.

Jobbik's popularity among Hungarians increased and in 2014, the party won 20.4% of the vote in the national elections, gleaning support from previous Fidesz voters.

Since then, far right political parties have experienced increased popularity also in France, Germany, Poland, Austria, Denmark and Slovakia, fuelled to a significant degree by local reaction to the influx of well over one million migrants from Syria, Iraq and other mostly Muslim nations from September 2015 onwards.

Renowned Holocaust researcher, the late Robert Wistrich, made the following comment, reported in the *Jerusalem Post* on July 7, 2014:

> "When a political party crosses the 20% threshold, they are a serious political force. The Jews of Europe do not have a future… I think their future is bleak."

Against this ominous prediction, as if to counter the weight of it, stands the story of Jane Haining. It seems, as mentioned in Part One of this book, that Jane's story will simply not 'lie down and die'.

Her testimony has been amazingly revived by the discovery in September, 2016, in an attic at the Church of Scotland headquarters in Edinburgh, of Jane's hand written will, dated 1942. A garnet ring belonging to Jane was also discovered in the small box.

No information as to how these found their way from Hungary to Scotland and into the attic is available, but it proves Jane was aware from early in the war years of her precarious position in Hungary, only adding to the awe her courage in remaining there inspires.

This discovery, once announced, 'went viral', being reported by media giants such as BBC, CNN, *The Guardian* (newspaper, UK),

and many other on-line news websites throughout the world -
surely an unusually strong media response to news about someone
who few people had ever heard of up until this point!

* * *

Author's note – some uncanny connections:

Back in 2011, after writing the first edition of this book, I was enjoying a hike close to the scenic town of Wanaka in New Zealand. I fell into conversation with another hiker who had lived in the same rural area in New Zealand as I had, as a young child.

The discussion revealed that a man that I remembered very vaguely (I was only 6 or 7 years old at the time), who had come to the tiny township of Dipton to fill in temporarily as pastor of the local Presbyterian Church, was in fact Rev George A F Knight - the same man who had been the director of the Scottish Mission to Budapest in Jane's day. I suddenly realised that I had actually met him, never thinking I would one day be writing a book in which he played a pivotal role. (His memoires were published in a book titled *What Next*.)

Another interesting discovery, post first edition publication, was that Frances Warburton Lee, Jane Haining's best foreign friend in Hungary, with whom she shared a prison cell, and from whose letters was gleaned valuable information about that period of Jane's life, was actually a New Zealander from Christchurch. It took the eagle eye of a Christchurch librarian to discover this connection in an old newspaper article during my visit to the library to do a presentation about Jane. Oddly enough, there is no documentary evidence that Jane knew of Frances' nationality. In fact she appeared to think she was British. Perhaps Frances was travelling on a British passport, but her family had been residents of Canterbury, New Zealand, for some generations, and Frances was brought up in New Zealand.

Appendix One:
Jane Haining's
chronological history

Family

Parents: Thomas John Haining, farmer, born 1866, in Glencairn, one of about five children to Thomas and Margaret Haining. Died June 10, 1922, in Dumfries Infirmary, aged fifty-five. Thomas John had four older sisters—all born in Glencairn. He was married in 1890, in Kirkcudbright, to Jane Mathison, born 1866 in Terregles, Kirkcudbrightshire.

Family lived at Dunscore on Lochenhead farm. Children: Alison Haining, born 1891, married James McKnight in 1918 and moved to Canada in 1926. Twin sons James and Thomas, born April, 1893, died August, 1893. Margaret Haining, born 1895, never married. Jane Mathison Haining, born June 6, 1897, at Lochenhead Farm. Helen Haining, born August, 1902.

Early deaths: Jane Mathison died in childbirth August 4, 1902, at age of thirty-six, at Lockenhead Farm. The young family help, Lily McShie, took on the role of looking after the family for two years, but after she married, cousin Margaret Fitzsimon took over this role.[16] Jane's sister Helen Haining, a weakly child, died on March 17, 1904, aged one and a half years.

Dunscore Village

Lochenhead Farm, at Throughgate, was a short walk from Dunscore Village, a thriving self-contained village with butcher, haberdasher, tailor, etc., in the early twentieth century. Thomas Haining also owned two houses in the village and one at Longbank, all of which were tenanted.[17] Lochenhead Farm and the farmhouse remain to this day.

Primary School

Jane attended Dunscore School until she was twelve years old. Her teacher, Miss Sloane, is described as "something of a martinet, strict in exacting obedience, but exceedingly kind."[18] The headmaster, Mr. Gold, also encouraged Jane to excel in her work. Little is known of her life outside school hours. After receiving excellent results in her scholarship examinations for Dumfries Academy, she joined her sister Margaret as a student there. The Dunscore School remains to this day, serving as a centre for preschool groups.

Church Life in Dunscore

The deeply pious family regularly attended Craig Free Church, formerly an old Reformed Presbyterian Church, situated just outside the village. Jane's father was a deacon and later an elder. He was also parish councillor, so the family was well aware of civic matters. Jane and her sisters were baptised here, and Jane attended Sunday school. Here, she learnt to love the Psalms of David.[19] The church was built by subscription and was closed in the 1950s. It is now a garage. A plinth outside the new Dunscore Church commemorates Jane's life.

Dumfries Academy

In 1909 Jane became a student at Dumfries Academy, a school with a fine reputation and some renowned former pupils, e.g. J. M. Barrie, who wrote *Peter Pan*.

The Moat Hostel for girls, the first of its kind in Scotland, had just opened that year. Jane became one of its first boarders.

At Dumfries Academy Jane was described as shy, retiring, and timid but with a propensity to mother other girls. School life was very full, with very little spare time outside of studies and school activities. On Sundays, the boarders would march in crocodile formation to the Buccleuch Street Church, where "she was inspired in her faith by Reverend Cairns."[20]

In her six years at the academy, Jane gained forty-one prizes, collecting seven in her first year and culminating in becoming modern dux (two duxes were selected each year) in her last year, 1915. She excelled in languages—Latin, French, and German. A photo in the school magazine shows Jane was a member of a girls' hockey team in her second to last year at the school. Female students were breaking new ground at the academy—the first female editor of the school magazine was appointed during Jane's time at the school.[21]

Working Life in Glasgow

In 1915, Jane left school and returned to Lochenhead farm to help out. In the autumn of 1915, Jane started a business course at the Athenaeum in Glasgow. Early in 1917, Jane graduated and took a temporary post before finding a position through the Athenaeum Employment Agency with J&P Coats Ltd., thread merchants in Paisley just outside Glasgow. Initially a clerk, she was quickly promoted to become a secretary and private secretary. She remained at J&P Coats for over ten years.

Church Life in Glasgow

Jane's rooms, at 90 Forth Street, Pollokshields, were quite near Queens Park West Church, which she attended regularly and to which she transferred her membership.

From 1917 onwards, Jane taught Sunday school on Sunday afternoons, was elected secretary of the Sunday school, and created a missions library for the church, possibly inspired by her cousin Margaret Colthart (a missionary to India under the auspices of a Canadian mission society). She also volunteered with the Band of Hope movement, which taught temperance and good Protestant values, and became a helper in the Congregational Mission in Cumberland Street.[22]

Father's Remarriage and Death

Jane's cousin, Margaret Fitzsimon, who had been running the household at Dunscore, left to get married, and Jane's sister Alison returned for a short time to take over.

In January 1922, Jane's father, Thomas Haining, married Roberta Maxwell, daughter of a neighbour living at Lochenlea Farm. He died on June 10 of that year. Roberta returned to her father's farm. In November 1922, Jane's half-sister Agnes was born.

The farm was sold, leaving Jane with only her rooms in Glasgow as a home. Her sister Margaret joined her in Glasgow for about five years.

Mission Focus

In 1927, Jane heard an address by the Church of Scotland Jewish Mission Committee convenor, Reverend Dr. George Mackenzie, about missionary work among the Jews of Central and Eastern Europe.

At the start of the 1930s, Jane attended a meeting of the committee and met Dr. Mackenzie. She offered her services to the cause. She told a friend, "I have found my life's work."[23] Jane attempted to resign her job but was persuaded by her employer, Mr. M. L. Peacock, to remain until he had recovered from an illness and until he could train someone else for her position. (In a letter dated 1936 to her cousin, Margaret Coltart, Jane confessed that she had had an ambition to have charge of a home for girls ever since her days in Glasgow.)[24]

Jane completed a diploma at the Glasgow School of Domestic Science and also a certificate in housekeeping, and then held several temporary positions, one in Glasgow and another in Manchester as matron at a radium institute.

In January 1932, Jane responded to an advertisement in the Church of Scotland magazine *Life and Work* for the position of matron of the girls' home at the Scottish Mission in Budapest. She held all qualifications necessary, including fluency in German and some musical ability.

On February 16, 1932, The Women's Jewish Mission Central Committee offered Jane the job. On March 7, Jane began her training at St. Colm's Women's Missionary College in Edinburgh and was given most satisfactory reports.[25] Jane reported in the letter to Margaret Coltart that she found God's guidance through natural ways rather than through the supernatural into this new work.

On June 19, 1932, Jane was dedicated for missionary work in a service held at St. Stephen's Church in Edinburgh.[26] The next day Jane set off for Budapest. She was now thirty-five years old.

Jewish Mission and Girls' Home

The Scottish Mission in Budapest, at Vörösmarty utca (Street) 51, in the centre of the city, was reputed to be the largest facility in the world dedicated to the evangelism of the Jews. Conversion was not forced on anyone—Hungarian law said only those over the age of eighteen could convert. All applicants for baptism had to take a six-week course in the tenets of the faith before their names were accepted.[27] The mission's school had a fine academic record.

In the summer of 1935, Jane took twelve of the girls' home girls to Lake Balaton, a favourite summer holiday place for Hungarians not far from Budapest, returning in September.

The school took in both Christians and Jews, who particularly valued the excellent standard of education. Later, during World War II, many Jews chose the school and girls' home as a place of refuge for their children.

In 1935, extracts from Jane's reports to the Women's Jewish Mission Council indicate the mission did not try to force conversions or even expect them, but provided a happy normal home environment, where Jewish children could discover and experience the love of God for themselves through the day to day example set by the Christian missionaries.[28]

Staff at Mission

In 1932, when Jane arrived, there was no matron. Margit Prém, headmistress at the Higher School had been carrying the load of both positions. There were only thirty boarders in the home, well below the average, while about 400 students attended the school. The school took students from age six to about fifteen or sixteen years old.[29] Jane took over the running of the home— purchasing food, hiring staff, and organising activities for boarders during out of school hours.

Scottish missionary in charge, Dr. William Beveridge, who had already resigned from his post, waited to welcome Jane.[30] His successor, Reverend John Calder, remained for three years.

In 1935, Reverend George A. F. Knight took over as missionary in charge.

In 1936, a Former Pupils Club was established so the mission could continue to support students, giving them teaching on the scriptures. A Girl Guide group was also established. Jane was now fluent in Hungarian, after receiving lessons from Miss Edith Roda, headmistress of the Elementary School.

Hitler Comes to Power in Germany

In January 1933, Hitler became Chancellor of Germany, and numerous anti-Semitic laws began to be passed in Germany and also in Hungary (see Appendix 2).

In 1934, in an attempt to counteract the rising anti-Semitism, and in line with the Church of Scotland's position against this, a series of lectures on the subject were organised in Budapest. These failed miserably as the media misquoted and misconstrued what lecturing pastors said and launched a vitriolic attack on the Scottish mission.[31]

In 1935, Jane took a two month furlough home, visiting the farm at Dunscore. On her return to Budapest, Jane instigated at home events on Sunday afternoons for former boarders and pupils. These reunions became a feature of the mission.

In 1937, Jane went on holiday with her sister Margaret to Switzerland. Germany invaded and annexed Austria in1938. Anti-Semitism increased in Hungary, and refugee children were now being accommodated in the girls' home. Jewish parents were asking Jane about ways to emigrate.[32]

In 1939, Jane took another furlough to the United Kingdom, this time with Margit Prém, visiting Glasgow, Aberdeen, and Galashiels to hold meetings. They then went to visit Jane's sister Margaret in Kent and on to Devon and Cornwall. Germany invaded Poland in 1939, and World War II began.

Back to Budapest

In the summer of 1939, Jane abandoned a plan to bring her half-sister Agnes back with her to Budapest because of the political situation. Jane and Margit Prém set off for Budapest on a nightmare journey, experiencing disrupted train connections and few services while travelling.[33]

Jane found a chaotic situation in Budapest, with some staff wanting to leave immediately and necessary supplies such as coal for heating and postal communications beginning to fail.

On May 10, 1940 mission director, Reverend Knight, was persuaded by the Scottish Mission to return with his family to the United Kingdom. He and some other staff members of the mission had been spied on for some time by the Nyilas (pro-Nazi Hungarian Arrow Cross movement). They had confronted him with their dossier about his alleged work for secret service agents, working undercover at the British Legation.[34]

A new mission council was formed under Dr. Alexander Nagy, Jane Haining, and Margit Prém.[35] This council continued to coordinate the mission's work in Budapest despite the increasing pressure of war and anti-Semitism.

On May 24, 1940, Jane refused to return to the United Kingdom, despite Jewish Mission Committee directives to do so. She told the committee she would take full responsibility for her decision. To further requests for her urgent return (prompted by the British evacuation at Dunkirk), she said it was not necessary, as there were still many British subjects living in Budapest, that she was in no danger, and that the girls' home was not suffering as much as other institutions as it enjoyed a degree of privilege.[36] Jane wrote, "If these children need me in days of sunshine how much more do they need me in days of darkness."[37]

By 1941, Hungary was now officially part of the Axis countries. Jane liaised with the Hungarian Reformed Church to ensure the mission continued to give shelter to the Jewish girls.

She kept in contact with Scotland through the Red Cross as well as the British and Swiss authorities.[38]

In 1942, Reverend Dr. Lajos Nagy, ordained minister of the Hungarian Reformed Church, became the acting head of the Scottish Mission to Budapest. And from 1942 to 1944, Jane became involved in pastoral care for British ex-patriots in Budapest, visiting, with Dr. Nagy, British prisoners of war who were being held in the southern part of Hungary, taking money, books, medicines, and even wireless sets into the camps.[39]

On March 19, 1944, Germany invaded Hungary. The British Foreign Office became concerned about Jane's safety.[40] The girls' home was filled to capacity. All Jews were now required to wear a yellow star, and it fell to Jane, with tears in her eyes, to sew these on the girls' uniforms.[41]

Arrest and Interrogation

About April 4, 1944, two Gestapo officers appeared at the mission, searched Jane's room and office, and gave her fifteen minutes to gather some belongings before taking her away. A number of staff and students witnessed her departure in a smart suit and with a smile on her face, saying she would be back soon. Some accounts say the Germans searched her bag and threw out her Bible, saying she would no longer need it. This Bible was later said to be found in the rubble of the girls' home, which was damaged in the siege of Budapest.

From this point on, information on events is less certain. Jane was taken either to one of several villas in the hills of Buda, which had been taken by the Gestapo from wealthy Jewish-Hungarian families as part of German SS commander Himmler's solution to the "Jewish problem"[42] or to the basement of the Gestapo headquarters in Hotel Majestic on Szabadsa Hill, then to a room in Hotel Belvedere.[43] The Gestapo took no notice whatsoever of the safe conduct pass issued to Jane by the Swiss legation. The arrest was ostensibly on suspicion of espionage.[44]

Probably at the end of April, Jane was then taken to Fö utca Prison[45] and there became a cellmate of Frances Warburton Lee, a New Zealand woman who had become a good friend of hers during the war years. Ms. Lee, in a letter to a cousin,[46] talked of the seventeen days Jane was imprisoned with her. She listed the charges Jane said had been levelled against her as:

1. She worked with the Jews.

2. She employed an Aryan housekeeper, whom she later dismissed.

3. She wept when the order came that all the children were to wear the yellow star.

4. She had English visitors.

5. She listened to the news from England on the BBC.

6. She visited the British prisoners on Count Andrássy's estate in the south of Hungary.

7. She had sent parcels to British prisoners of war.

8. She was active in politics.

Jane's responses, recorded by Miss Lee:

1. Her work at the Scottish Mission necessitated working with Jews.

2. The housekeeper came of her own free will and had nothing to do with the children. Her dismissal was required under the new law, which said an Aryan could not be employed in a household where Jews lived. (Jane had given her a generous severance payment and helped her find another position.)[47]

3. Yes, she wept as she sewed on the stars—Jane wept at the memory of it, and the officers interrogating her left the room until she regained her composure.

4. Naturally, she had visitors from Britain.

5. She was obliged to have a wireless set, as she had a responsibility to the mission children and needed to hear the air raid warnings.

6. The Hungarian Count had given Dr. Nagy and herself permission to visit the prisoner of war camp there at Christmastime to hold a service.

7. The Hungarian Government had given her permission to send parcels to the prisoners.

8. She vehemently denied she had ever talked politics or meddled in politics.

Ms. Lee reported Jane being taken twice for questioning by the Gestapo. She had not returned dismayed from these sessions, seemingly expecting the Germans to see the ridiculous nature of the accusations.

Jane confided in Miss Lee that the Germans had asked if she knew who had denounced her, and she suggested the son-in-law of her housekeeper and cook (Mrs. Kovacs) named Schréder, who was a member of the fascist Arrow Cross movement. Jane had refused to allow him to stay overnight at the mission and confronted him about eating mission food. The interrogator indicated to her she may well be correct in her assumption.[48]

Hungarian Reformed Church Bishop Ravasz and Miklos Mester (state counsellor at the Hungarian Ministry of Education and a leading figure in the underground activities of the secretly organised movement of national resistance) approached local officials and put their case to the premier as well as the regent, Admiral Horthy. The Bishop offered to guarantee her containment in the deaconess's home if they would release her. According to a letter written by Reverend Alexis Mathe to Reverend Alex King in 1946, the regent became very angry and ordered the Minister of Foreign Affairs to secure her release.[49]

The Germans refused to say where Jane was being held. Jane was found at Fö utca Prison by chance as her friends went from prison to prison with a food parcel for her. During her imprisonment, they were able to bring her two parcels, but when they brought the third, they found she had been moved on.

Deportation and Death

Early in May, 1944, Jane was moved from Fö utca Prison to a holding camp, Kistarcsa, twenty-five kilometres from Budapest. Ms. Lee's letter stated that the other prisoners had been delighted for Jane, as they imagined the conditions there would be vastly superior to the prison.

On May 15, 1944, Jane was placed with about ninety other Hungarian women prisoners in cattle wagons in a train bound for Auschwitz-Birkenau Concentration Camp in Upper Silesia. This was not strictly a Jewish transport. She was incarcerated in Birkenau, tattooed with the number 79467, and given the designation political prisoner.[50]

Little is known of the following events. The mission learnt of her incarceration in Auschwitz-Birkenau from post cards she sent. (She sent two, the last dated July 15, two days before she died.)[51] Prisoners were allowed to send postcards only in German and written in pencil. Jane's German was sufficiently good for her to take advantage of this.

The majority of prisoners transported from Hungary with Jane would have gone straight from the train to the gas chambers, as most would have been Jews and they were destined for immediate extermination at Birkenau, but Jane must have been selected to live as she got off the train.

On July 17, 1944, Jane Haining died, ostensibly from cachexia, while in hospital in Birkenau.

On August 2, 1944, British officials were informed that Jane was in Auschwitz.

August 17, 1944, British officials learned of her death. The official death certificate, sent to the German Legation in Budapest and forwarded on to the Swiss Government, stated Jane, "who was arrested on justifiable suspicion of espionage against Germany, died in hospital, July 17, of cachexia, following intestinal catarrh."[52]

Cachexia is a general collapse of the bodily organs due to starvation or a chronic illness. No evidence has been found that this stated cause of death was in fact the correct one.

On August 22, 1944, a Gestapo official called at the Scottish Mission with a bundle of Jane's personal effects and papers, reporting Jane had died of natural causes.

On September 12, 1944, The British Red Cross wrote to the Jewish Mission Committee expressing its sympathy on the death of Jane and stating it had received a telegram from Margit Prém, recording Jane's presence in Auschwitz.

The British Foreign Office responded to the news of her death by promising to investigate the exact cause and, should ill-treatment have been the cause, to bring those responsible to justice.[53] In August 1944, Margit Prém died after becoming very melancholic following Jane's departure. (Letter from Reverend Alex Mathe, dated 29.7.1946, to Rev Alex King.)[54] Many believe the real reason for Jane's arrest and incarceration (leading to her death) was not because of suspicion of espionage, but because of her role in working with the Jews.

In October of 1944, The Church of Scotland World Mission's Jewish Committee adopted a minute stating, "When Germany occupied Hungary in April, 1944, she was not long in coming under their notice as an opponent of anti-Semitism and a lover of Israel."[55]

Commemoration

Jane's Bible, supposedly found in the midst of rubble of the girls' home contained a bookmark given to her by one of the girls, with a scripture which provides the perfect postscript for her life. It stated, "Be not afraid, only believe. Mark 5:36."

Two short memorial services were held for Jane, one in St. George's West Church in Edinburgh, conducted by Reverend W. W. Gauld and Reverend Dr. James Black on September 28, 1944, and another in Budapest conducted by Reverend Knight on June 30, 1946.

On May 16, 1948, two stained glass windows, named Service (with the inscription heading Feed My Lambs) and Sacrifice (with the inscription heading Greater Love Hath No Man), were unveiled at Queens Park West Church in Glasgow in her memory.

In 1984, The Scottish Mission marked the fortieth anniversary of Jane's death with a service and reminiscences from former students. The Jewish community in Budapest erected a marble plaque in the Scottish Mission in her memory.

In 1990, the Israeli ambassador to Hungary presented a certificate to the mission to mark the planting of a memorial tree for Jane in the Jerusalem hills.

In 1994, The Scottish Mission marked the fiftieth anniversary of her death with a memorial service.

On December 8, 1997, Jane's memory was honoured by Yad Vashem in a posthumous presentation of a Righteous Among the Nations certificate and medal to Jane's half-sister, Mrs. Agnes

O'Brien (nee Haining), by the Israeli ambassador to United Kingdom, Mr. Moshe Raviv. The medal and certificate now reside at the St. Mungo Museum of Religious Life and Art in Glasgow.

Yad Vashem is the Holocaust martyrs' and heroes' remembrance authority in Jerusalem whose mission is to preserve the memory of martyrs of the Holocaust for all time to come through exhibitions, research, and education programmes. Jane Haining is the only Scot to be presented a Righteous Among the Nations award. Jane's name has been added to the Wall of Remembrance.

A cairn has also been erected in front of the new church in Dunscore in Jane's honour. In 2010, the Jewish community of Budapest hosted for the first time a conference in Jane's honour. Jane's Bible was found hidden in a safe at St. Columba's Church, Budapest.

In September, 2016, Jane's hand written will, dated 1944, was found in the attic of the Church of Scotland headquarters in Edinburgh, along with a garnet ring.

Appendix Two:
Hungary and
Its Anti-Semitic Laws

What follows is an overview of Hungary's extremely ambivalent attitude to its large Jewish population, through the eyes of Holocaust survivors Mordechai Reuveni, born in 1923 in Budapest, and died in 2016 in Israel, and his wife Chavah, now living in Nazareth, Israel.[56]

> Anti-Semitism, which peaked during World War Two, has been no stranger to Hungary. During the war, it resulted in the deaths of about 400,000 of its Jewish population of 600,000 through deportation to concentration camps, on death marches to work camps, or through assignment to the Russian front, sometimes without weapons.
>
> The Jews have a long history in the Carpathian basin which was to become the nation of Hungary. Some are believed to have fled there after the fall of the second temple in Jerusalem in 70 CE. Until 1867, the Jews were not allowed to become citizens of the country, but in that year Franz Joseph II, ruler of the Austria-Hungarian Empire gave them their emancipation. By 1914, Jews made up about one million of Hungary's total population of 18 million.
>
> Hungary had evolved a feudal system with land-owning nobles retaining power. However, Jews became more educated and

began to prosper, opening factories and gaining economic power. After the 1917 Communist revolution in Russia, things changed. There was a popular leftist uprising in Hungary in 1919, led by Bela Kun. Both wealthy Jews and Gentiles alike were persecuted during this period, if they did not support the rebellion.

Admiral Horthy from the Hungarian/Austrian Navy suppressed the rebellion with the help of Czech and Romanian forces, and took over as regent. As many of the leaders in Bela Kun's party were Jews, the Jewish people became targets for rising anti-Jewish/anti-Communist feeling.

"Those Jews who supported the communist uprising turned against their own people, trying to be 'more communist than the communists'," Hungarian Holocaust survivor Mordechai Reuveni of Nazareth, Israel, says. "After the uprising there was a five year period in which Jews were assaulted and murdered."

In 1920, a law was passed stating only 20 percent of Jews could study at university. The Jews found they could live with this level of discrimination. In 1927, anti-Semitism abated somewhat and Hungary became a relative haven for the Jews of Europe. The Hungarian Zionist Organisation was again ratified.

However, in 1938, laws limited trading with Jews and their employment. The First Jewish Law introduced a quota system, limiting Jewish participation in the professions and business to 20 percent.

Mr. Reuveni remembers: "My mother was a home maker until then, but she had to go to work. My father was fired from his position as newspaper proof reader because he was a Jew, and both had to work in a factory in lowly jobs. Jews were no longer allowed to work in professional positions."

More laws followed. Jews were not allowed to work in government positions either. Factories owned by Jews were nationalised and a non-Jew was placed in top management. The Jews no longer had access to the profits from their businesses.

In the early years, any anti-Semitic reactions were based on religion, but later they became based on ethnicity, so that Jews who had converted to Christianity were also included in the 'Jewish Laws.'

In 1939, a Second Jewish Law reduced Jewish participation in the professions, industry and commerce to only five percent. Jews were now classified as anyone born to Jewish parents, or two or more Jewish grandparents, whether they had converted to another religion or not. About 250,000 Jews lost their source of livelihood.

On November 20, 1940, Hungary signed the Tripartite Pact, effectively joining the Axis powers in the war against United Kingdom and its allies. This was prompted by Hungary's increasing economic dependence on the Axis states and desire to regain territories lost after WWI.

In 1941, Hungary signed an agreement with Hitler in which he agreed not to attack Hungary, and promised to give back about two thirds of its territory lost after a disastrous coalition with Austria in World War I, leading to its defeat along with Germany. Two weeks after Hungary signed a peace agreement with Yugoslavia, Hitler was demanding access through Hungary to attack Yugoslavia. The Hungarian Prime Minister Pál Teleki, committed suicide, presumably as an act of regret for the inability of Hungary to stand against the pressure from Germany.

The same year the Hungarian government sent large numbers of poorly equipped Jews to the Russian front to support the

Nazi push to the east. Jews were required to wear a yellow stripe on their uniform and Jewish converts to Christianity a white stripe. About 35,000 Jews died there. During this period Mr. Reuveni and countless other Jewish citizens went into hiding, living from hand to mouth, smuggling or stealing, using false papers which declared them to be Christians, and relying on Christian friends or individuals with influence from neutral countries for shelter, and to avoid induction into work camps or the army.

A Third Jewish Law was passed prohibiting Jews from marrying 'Aryans' and also providing stiff penalties for sexual relations between the two groups.

The Jews had generally believed that this was a passing phase and things would eventually get better, but the opposite was soon seen to be true. A Hungarian fascist movement, the (Nyilas) Arrow Cross, an ultra-right group intent on destroying the Hungarian Jewish population, now began to gain much power. Formed in 1935, it had ingratiated itself with its Nazi mentors.

The new prime minister, Miklós Kállay, initially went along with German policies, ordering in 1942 the expropriation of Jewish property and further restrictions on economic and cultural life of Jews. At this time, Germany was calling for the introduction of "the final solution to the Jewish problem" and asking Hungary to 'resettle' the 800,000 Hungarian-speaking Jews from the now wider area of Hungarian influence.

By 1943, Kállay had realised that the Allies would win the war and was trying to back away from supporting the Nazi war initiative. He attempted to make contact with the Allies to inform them of his new position. Hungary toned down its anti- Jewish rhetoric and allowed the press to operate with relative freedom. Leftist political parties were allowed to exist.

In 1944, Hungary faced the advance and imminent invasion of the Russian forces.

Realising this, and concerned about the 'softening' of Hungary's political stance, the Nazis broke their 1941 peace agreement and invaded Hungary in March, 1944. Gestapo officer, Adolf Eichmann, who was responsible for organising the transportation of Jews from around Europe to extermination camps, came personally to Hungary to put into action 'the final solution' for the Jews.

A new government was formed with a puppet Hungarian prime minister, but the Nazi ambassador held all the power. All Jews now had to wear yellow stars and all wealthy Jews were arrested.

Securing the cooperation of the Hungarian 'gendarmerie', the Germans immediately began to make lists of all rural Jews and in April, 1944, Hungarian troops, at the behest of the Nazis, began to gather them together in village ghettos. Here they were put to work, mostly in old brick factories. In Budapest, Jews were not initially put into ghettos, but were required to live in designated buildings, with Hungarian residents having to move out to make way for the Jews.

"In early June, 1944, they started to send the Jews to a place no-one knew where," remembers Mr. Reuveni's wife Chavah, who was one of the rural Jews herded with her family into a ghetto and then packed into a cattle truck and sent by train to work camps. "I was in a train that went to Austria."

The entire population of rural Jews was deported, either to work camps, or to Auschwitz Concentration Camp for extermination.

The Interior Ministry created two ghettos for Budapest Jews, the Big Ghetto in what is now the Jewish Quarter of Pest, and the International Ghetto, to the north. The urban Jews were mostly herded into these two ghettos. Some hid in Christian homes or with friends or remained in designated 'safe houses'.

Neutral countries such as Switzerland, Spain and Sweden, finally realising the horrific intentions of the Nazis, started issuing papers to Jews stating they came under their protection. The Nazis paid little attention to these papers. Jews were arrested by the Germans with the help of their protegees, the Nyilas, shot, and their bodies thrown into the River Duna (Danube).

"The Nazis demanded Hungary send 50,000 people to work in Austria and so the Hungarians collected this number from the ghettos. As all the men aged between 19 and 45 were already in the army, it was women, children and old people they took," says Mr. Reuveni. "They had to march by foot all the way. I was caught in May 1944 and was sent to an army work camp in Hungary. I met my mother and sister 125 kilometres from Budapest, as their convoy marched on its way to Vienna. I also later met my father and was able to help him escape from his convoy." Mr. Reuveni escaped from his work party, was caught, and faced a firing squad but was amazingly only injured. Someone rescued him and he spent a short time in hospital in Budapest before crawling away to find his family. In the process he saw many signs of the atrocities being committed in the city, including the bodies of murdered citizens lying frozen under the winter ice.

On January 18, 1945, Pest was liberated by the Russian army. By then, Mr. Reuveni had joined the Krasnaya Guardia (Hungarian Red Guard).

"But I never agreed with communism – it's against my nature," he says.

On February 12, 1945, he escaped from his militia unit and fled to the Romanian capital Bucharest, eventually making his way to Israel where he still remembers with great clarity the years of his youth in Budapest, under the anti-Semitic Hungarian regime.

Most of Budapest's Jews survived the war but there was barely a single survivor amongst the much larger rural Jewish population.

Appendix Three:
Some Quotes By Those
Who Knew Jane Haining

The following are quotes from some of those who knew Jane Haining during the twelve years she worked in Budapest at the Scottish Mission to the Jews.

> Reverend Robert Smith BD, from Prague, who with his wife, visited Budapest and the mission in 1936:

I thought she was a fine example of a Scot abroad—with her sonsy face and cheery smile and unmistakable accent, and yet so completely at home in Hungary that you wondered which country she loved more.

Mrs Smith added:

Jane Haining—a real mother to all the girls under her care.[57]

Anna (surname unknown), a student during 1944, who wrote in a letter shortly after Jane's arrest:

Then she was taken away. I still feel tears in my eyes and hear in my ears the siren of the Gestapo motor-car. I see the smile on her face while she bade farewell. ...I never saw Miss Haining again, and when I went to the Scottish Mission to ask the minister about her, I was told she had died. I didn't want to believe or to understand it, but a long time later I realised that she had died for me and for others ... I will never forget Miss Haining, and I will try to follow in her footsteps.[58]

Bertalan Tamás, pastor with the Scottish Mission from 1980, collected reminiscences of former students of the Scottish Mission and presented them at an Advent service in St. Columba's Church in 1985. He commented:

Here in the Scottish Mission, no efforts were made to achieve spectacular (*conversion* - author's addition for clarification) results. Rather, souls affected souls.

Report on Advent Service at the Scottish Mission, 1985

The following are quotes from past teachers and students about Jane Haining and the Scottish Mission and Girls' Home, gathered together in the 1985 booklet of reminiscences:

Ibolya Gsengery, student and after 1948, teacher, at the mission:

Thanks to the Scottish Mission, I had strength for everything. Here I was given the foundation, I mean faith and composure, that remained with me for the rest of my life.

Emma Horváth (Mrs. Boros), teacher from 1921:

Our martyred colleague, Miss Haining, a lovable personality, made the girls' home a warm home indeed, thus those years are still well remembered. The school and Scottish and Hungarian mission activities earned respect all over the country. ... Our youth were characterized by a solid trust in God and by following Christ in charity.

Henrietta Bartos, a student pre-1939:

I lived in the girls' home for eight years. Every morning we studied the Bible in our class. We read a section of the New and Old Testament and sang psalms. I also attended Sunday school. I was a girl scout and was a patrol leader. We made a lot of excursions, camped at Tahi and Dravapalkonya. After the war, I completed my studies and taught at state run schools. I wanted to pass on the love I had received (*at the mission school –* author's addition for clarification) in my childhood.

Edith Charatán (Mrs. Terényi), student from 1940 or 1941:

Faith wasn't forced upon anybody. I was as much interested in the reformed Bible lessons as in the Jewish religion. I got best marks in both. What we were taught at school enabled us to live up to our commitments, to make a living until we retired. In spite of the historic days, we lived in a peaceful, protected atmosphere.

Sophie Sütö (Mrs Parragh), employee of the mission:

A shining ray of light—that was the years I worked at the mission. On my first night there, Miss Haining brought my supper to my room as I did not yet know my way around. ...Then in 1944, I saw when Miss Haining was seized and the girls disappeared one by one. The war swept our former happy days far, far away. Now I glance back and return (to visit the Scottish Mission) for morsels, for corn.

Elisabeth Somogyi (Mrs Dr. Séllyei) student from 1935:

At the beginning of the term in 1935/36, probably on the last day of August, three girls ascended the stairs of the Scottish Mission school. The door was opened and Miss Haining appeared. We saw her smiling face, her warm glance through her eyeglasses. After saying farewell, our parents disappeared and the three of us hung our heads in sorrow. My eldest sister Marianne did not cry, but Margaret and I burst into tears. Miss Haining took our hands in hers and introduced us to our school mates.

Crying was replaced by curiosity and showing off.

Susannah Spiegel (Mrs Korányi), student from 1939 to 1944:

As long as possible, until March 19, 1944, the day of the German occupation, everything, all the dreadful events were kept outside these (mission) walls. We were children, equals (Jewish and Christian) and nothing else but knowledge counted.

Julianna Gzurja (Mrs Magyar), student from 1934 to 1938:

Our beloved Miss Haining made us grow used to order and discipline. She read the Bible to us in English and German after every supper and she taught us the Lord's Prayer in German and English.

Ibolya Vadász (Mrs Garma's), student from 1936:

I was lucky to spend some years with Miss Haining. At the time, I felt like a martyr as we had to wear black stockings, and the drills seemed like being in a prison. But as an adult, I am grateful for the Spartan way of life as that has helped me through a lot of hardships.

Clara Szücs (Mrs Tamar Weiss), student from 1938 to 1942:

From 1938 to 1942, I had a happy peaceful childhood. Anti-Semitism presented itself in many places and forms in those times, but within the Scottish school, I never sensed it either from the teachers or another student, either directly or indirectly. The Scotch was a warm nest. In the upper school classes, I gained morally, and that lasts a life time.

Endnotes

1. Exact words written on the bookmark. The Bible translation the child took this from was not recorded.

2. Pengo was the currency introduced to Hungary in the post World War I period when the Austria Hungarian Empire was dismantled. It suffered enormous inflation at the end of World War II and was replaced by the forint, still the currency of Hungary in 2017.

3. Holy Spirit

4. Roman Catholic Sister Sára Salkaházi, a member of the Sisters of Social Service, made a commitment to set up a safe house for Jewish families. An informant led Nyilas supporters to the house in December, 1944, and she, along with all the occupants and some co-workers, was taken to the banks of the Danube River and shot

5. The Italian was Giorgio Perlasca who had fought in the Spanish Civil War and because of this had gained Spanish nationality. He used his nationality to step into the breach when the Spanish consul left, to aid in the rescue of Jews through Spanish diplomatic channels.

6. man = "manna." In the Complete Jewish Bible, it is written as the Hebrew word *man*.

7. Kosher foods are those which conform to the rules of Judaism.

8. The Lord my God

9. Yahweh or Jehovah

10. Jerusalem

11. Zion

12. Judah

13. Original letter in Church of Scotland's Jane Haining archive at the National Library of Scotland, Edinburgh.

14. illegible word

15. *Jane Haining and the Work of the Scottish Mission with Hungarian Jews, 1932 – 1945:* Nicholas Railton: Available from St Columba's Church, Vorosmarty utca 51, 1064 B, Budapest.

16. Information sourced from *Jane Haining 1897 – 1944*; Revd David McDougall, MA, PhD, Edinburgh, 1953; edited and updated: Ian Alexander, 1998.

17. Council records, Dumfries Public Library.

18. Information sourced from *Jane Haining 1897 – 1944*; Revd David McDougall, MA, PhD, Edinburgh, 1953; edited and updated: Ian Alexander, 1998.

19. Ibid.

20. Information sourced from *Jane Haining and the Work of the Scottish Mission with Hungarian Jews, 1932 – 1945*, Nicholas Railton, 2007.

21. Dumfries Academy former pupils' magazine *The Minerva Magasine*, 1996 issue 2, Dumfries Public Library.

22. Information sourced from *Jane Haining and the Work of the Scottish Mission with Hungarian Jews, 1932 – 1945*, Nicholas Railton, 2007.

23. Information sourced from *Jane Haining 1897 – 1944*; Revd David McDougall, MA, PhD, Edinburgh, 1953; edited and updated: Ian Alexander, 1998.

24. Information sourced from *Jane Haining and the Work of the Scottish Mission with Hungarian Jews, 1932 – 1945*, Nicholas Railton, 2007.

25. Ibid.

26. Ibid.

27. Ibid.

28. Church of Scotland World Mission archives, Edinburgh.

29. Information sourced from *Jane Haining and the Work of the Scottish Mission with Hungarian Jews, 1932 – 1945*, Nicholas Railton, 2007.

30. Information sourced from *Jane Haining 1897 – 1944*; Revd David McDougall, MA, PhD, Edinburgh, 1953; edited and updated: Ian Alexander, 1998

31. Information sourced from *Jane Haining and the Work of the Scottish Mission with Hungarian Jews, 1932 – 1945*, Nicholas Railton, 2007.

32. Ibid.

33. Information sourced from *Jane Haining 1897 – 1944*; Revd David McDougall, MA, PhD, Edinburgh, 1953; edited and updated: Ian Alexander, 1998.

34. Information sourced from *Jane Haining and the Work of the Scottish Mission with Hungarian Jews, 1932 – 1945*, Nicholas Railton, 2007.

35. Ibid.

36. Ibid.

37. Information sourced from *Jane Haining 1897 – 1944*; Revd David McDougall, MA, PhD, Edinburgh, 1953; edited and updated: Ian Alexander, 1998.

38. Information sourced from *Jane Haining and the Work of the Scottish Mission with Hungarian Jews, 1932 – 1945*, Nicholas Railton, 2007.

39. Ibid.

40. Information sourced from *Jane Haining 1897 – 1944*; Revd David McDougall, MA, PhD, Edinburgh, 1953; edited and updated: Ian Alexander, 1998.

41. Ibid.

42. Ibid.

43. Information sourced from *Jane Haining and the Work of the Scottish Mission with Hungarian Jews, 1932 – 1945*, Nicholas Railton, 2007.

44. Ibid.

45. Official Auschwitz records.

46. Church of Scotland World Mission archives, Edinburgh.

47. Information sourced from *Jane Haining 1897 – 1944*; Revd David McDougall, MA, PhD, Edinburgh, 1953; edited and updated: Ian Alexander, 1998.

48. Information sourced from *Jane Haining and the Work of the Scottish Mission with Hungarian Jews, 1932 – 1945*, Nicholas Railton, 2007.

49. Church of Scotland World Mission archives, Edinburgh.

50. Official Auschwitz records.

51. National Library of Scotland archives, Edinburgh.

52. Information sourced from *Jane Haining and the Work of the Scottish Mission with Hungarian Jews, 1932 – 1945*, Nicholas Railton, 2007.

53. Ibid.

54. Church of Scotland World Mission archives, Edinburgh.

55. Information sourced from *Jane Haining and the Work of the Scottish Mission with Hungarian Jews, 1932 – 1945*, Nicholas Railton, 2007.

56. (Further historic facts may be found in Encyclopaedia Judaica (1971): Hungary, Vol. 8, col. 1103, online.)

57. *Jane Haining*, by Reverend David McDougall, page 19

58. *Jane Haining*, by Reverend David McDougall, page 32

Lightning Source UK Ltd.
Milton Keynes UK
UKHW040643170122
397266UK00001B/13

9 781911 211358